"*The Girl in the Middle* speaks directly to women navigating life's in-between seasons. Emma Mae McDaniel meets you where you are while gently calling you forward. Her heart is refreshingly pure, which you feel as she shares her personal story of anxiety and search for peace. She is equipping a generation of girls to use God's Word and His wisdom, using real-life examples to encourage and help transform anyone in any season."

—Oneka McClellan, lead pastor at Shoreline City Church

"*The Girl in the Middle* is such a beautiful overflow of Emma's heart—full of joy, life, and deep love for Jesus. Her words remind you that you're not alone in the in-between, and that freedom is found not in getting it all right, but in walking closely with Him. This book will inspire you and anchor you in real truth to live out life with Jesus with boldness and joy."

—Laney Rene, founder of The One He Loves ministry

"Reading this book feels like sitting across from Emma Mae at a coffee shop—being encouraged, poured into, and gently pointed to Christ. *The Girl in the Middle* equips you to face big decisions with boldness, grounded in grace and truth. Whether you're standing at a crossroads or see one coming ahead, Emma beautifully shows the power of walking in step with the Spirit, even in the most confusing or chaotic seasons of life."

—Allyson Golden, author of *Arise and Shine*

"In this book, you'll learn how to find true confidence in Christ that will change your life and your perspective. Emma reminds us that following Jesus truly changes everything. All young women need this book, and if they read it, they'll leave changed."

—GRACE VALENTINE, bestselling author, speaker, and
podcast host of *Water into Wine*

"Emma's knowledge and wisdom given from the Lord are all over this book. *The Girl in the Middle* will help any girl fall deeper in love with the Lord and know how to go all in with Him."

—JEANINE AMAPOLA WARD, author, Christian influencer, and
podcast host of *Happy & Healthy*

"Emma's boldness, even in the face of hurt, will stir something deep in your heart. She shows what it means to choose Christ over comfort, and, y'all, it's powerful. If you're ready to stop living halfway and go all in with Jesus, *The Girl in the Middle* is your next read."

—SADIE ROBERTSON HUFF, speaker, author, and
founder of Live Original

"Emma writes with joy, honesty, and conviction as she invites you to truly live out faith in a practical way. *The Girl in the Middle* will compel you toward Christ and give you the confidence to choose Truth whenever you're stuck in the middle of faith and fear."

—JORDAN LEE DOOLEY, bestselling author of
Own Your Everyday

"Emma Mae's perspective and example are exactly what I want for myself and the women in my life: my daughters, my friends, those I get to lead, and those I am being led by. *The Girl in the Middle* will make us stronger and sweeter as we chase and trust Jesus together. Thank you, Emma Mae, for this brave and beautiful offering."

—DONNA STUART, daughter of the King, wife, mother, mentor,
friend at Passion City Church in Washington, D.C.

THE GIRL
IN THE
MIDDLE

THE GIRL
IN THE
MIDDLE

CHOOSING TO LIVE OUT
YOUR FAITH IN THE EVERYDAY

EMMA MAE
McDANIEL

WATERBROOK

WaterBrook
An imprint of the Penguin Random House Christian Publishing Group,
a division of Penguin Random House LLC
1745 Broadway, New York, NY 10019
waterbrookmultnomah.com
penguinrandomhouse.com

LIBRARY OF CONGRESS CATALOGING-IN-PUBLICATION DATA
Names: McDaniel, Emma Mae, author
Title: The girl in the middle: choosing to live out your faith in the everyday / Emma Mae McDaniel.
Description: First edition. | New York, NY: WaterBrook | Includes bibliographical references.
Identifiers: LCCN 2024060674 | ISBN 9780593602485 hardcover | ISBN 9780593602492 ebook
Subjects: LCSH: Christian life—Biblical teaching | God (Christianity)—Love—Biblical teaching | Bible—Criticism, interpretation, etc.
Classification: LCC BS680.C44 M33 2025 | DDC 248.8/33—dc23/eng/20250620
LC record available at https://lccn.loc.gov/2024060674

Printed in the United States of America on acid-free paper

1st Printing

First Edition

BOOK TEAM: Production editor: Jocelyn Kiker • Managing editor: Julia Wallace
Production manager: Katie Zilberman • Copy editor: Michael Burke
Proofreaders: Debbie Anderson, Julia Henderson • Editor: Susan Tjaden

The authorized representative in the EU for product safety and compliance is Penguin Random House Ireland, Morrison Chambers, 32 Nassau Street, Dublin D02 YH68, Ireland. https://eu-contact.penguin.ie

For details on special quantity discounts for bulk purchases, contact specialmarketscms@penguinrandomhouse.com.

To my incredible husband, the one who walked with me,
encouraged me, and prayed for me steadily
as the message of this book was written.

CONTENTS

THE GIRL
IN THE
MIDDLE

1

Middle Moments

Millions call themselves by His name, it is true, and pay some token homage to Him, but a simple test will show how little He is really honored among them. Let the average man be put to the proof on the question of who or what is above, and his true position will be exposed. Let him be forced into making a choice between God and money, between God and men, between God and personal ambition, God and self, God and human love, and God will take second place every time. Those other things will be exalted above. However the man may protest, the proof is in the choice he makes day after day throughout his life.

—A. W. Tozer

When I was fourteen, I found myself overwhelmed by an ongoing struggle to keep anxious thoughts from taking over. Though I fought hard, I felt like I was losing the intense war for peace in my mind. I was worn out, missing the simpler days when it seemed like I didn't have a worry in the world. I remember one particular night when my chest was pounding and my nerves felt as tense as they could possibly be all throughout my body. I wondered, *Where is peace? Why am I grappling so hard to find it but finding myself empty-handed over and over again?* I couldn't carry the weight of the fear any longer, but the problem was that I didn't know where to put all my spiraling thoughts. So I continued lugging the burden around, almost convinced that was just how my life was going to be.

That night, as I sat crying at the foot of my bed, my dad walked into my room, checking to see how I was doing. With deep love, he patiently listened as I stumbled over my words, trying to articulate the exhausting internal conflict I was in. After we talked for a little bit about the fear that was stealing my joy, he turned to my bookshelf and pointed at my Bible that was stacked against fifty other books. He asked, "Emma, when was the last time you carved out space to be alone with God, reading His Word?"

"I honestly don't know," I said. I knew a lot about God, having grown up in the church and having been raised by parents who loved Him. I didn't personally know Him, though. "I can't think of the last time I sat with God by myself and read the Bible," I said.

"Emma, when Jesus comes back, I will not be standing beside you, holding your hand. It will be just you and Him," he said. "He will either tell you, 'Well done, good and faithful servant,' or 'I never knew you; depart from me'" (Matthew 25:21; Matthew 7:23).

My dad then left the room, and I sat on my bed pondering what he said. I knew that in that moment, I was in the company of both God and the anxiety that had been like a dense fog so cumbersome on my soul. Reflecting on the words my dad had spoken and feeling the pursuing love of God drawing me close, I decided to give my life to Jesus that night, telling God that I wanted to know Him more than anything else. My tears of heaviness were joined with tears of hope and light all at once. My chest, which had been pounding with worry, was now beating with a strange joy, an awareness that in that moment things were different. I knew that even in the fears and anxiety, I had been given the victory in Christ in that very instant. The journey of learning to walk in full freedom was just beginning for me, all because of Jesus. I was confident that I was not alone. My soul had a friend in God. I knew He was with me. I didn't have to wait for the mess of fear and anxiety to get cleaned up to experience His joy. He met me in my mess and loved me that night.

FILLED WITH THE WORD
AND OVERFLOWING WITH LOVE

For the next two years I immersed myself in the Bible. I set my alarm early enough so that I could have time before school to talk with God and read His Word. Being with Him before doing anything else set the tone of my whole day. I taped notecards with Scripture written on them all over my room. To memorize God's words, I would strategically place the notecards next to things associated with whatever verse was written on them. On my lamp, I taped Psalm 119:105: "Your word is a lamp to my feet and a light to my path." I stuck Psalm 4:8 on my bed frame: "In peace I will both lie down and sleep; for you alone, O LORD, make me dwell in safety." I placed Proverbs 31:25 on my closet door: "Strength and dignity are her clothing, and she laughs at the time to come." Romans 1:16 hung on my door so I could see it right before I stepped out of my room and into my day: "For I am not ashamed of the gospel, for it is the power of God for salvation to everyone who believes."

Before long, I realized these words breathed by God were not just written down on notecards and taped all over my bedroom. Surely enough, because I was regularly seeing them and thinking on them throughout the day, these Bible verses were being written on my heart, to have with me moment by moment. The Scriptures were guiding me, comforting me, and equipping me in my daily life, helping me navigate how to treat those around me and even how to process through my own anxious thoughts. Through God's Word, I learned who He is and who I am in Him. I discovered that the life He called me to had a purpose bigger than myself. Because my life was eternally changed by Christ, the way I lived my life daily in the here and now would never be the same. He filled me with joy that can only be found in His presence.

Personally knowing Him motivated me with the desire to make Him known to as many people as possible. As I was filled with eagerness to share Christ in any space I could, the Holy Spirit prompted me to start intentionally leveraging my Instagram account for the purpose of encouraging people and telling them about Christ. I changed my Instagram name from "emmamaej99" to "1corinthians13_love" because it was a simple way to say that my life wasn't about me anymore, it was all about Him. I wanted to help people know His love that would never fail them. I wanted to lead people to have a genuine relationship with Him. Even if someone simply came across my account, only catching a glimpse of my username, I hoped that they would be drawn to His heart through it.

Rarely would I be writing a caption to post and not be cut off by the red bar that read "Caption too long." The maximum number of words Instagram allowed had been surpassed. Yet, the 2,200-character limit couldn't contain the words of life bubbling over from within me. My cup truly was overflowing! I had so much to say because I loved God so much and He was changing my life.

Each day, I sought out opportunities to have a conversation with somebody and encourage them in the truth, because reading the Bible didn't only impact me, but it also compelled me to share its impact with others. As each day passed, I felt more and more discontent at the thought of keeping to myself this light that had shined in my own darkness. I empathized with the prophet Jeremiah, who wrote, "If I say, 'I will not mention him, or speak any more in his name,' there is in my heart as it were a burning fire shut up in my bones, and I am weary with holding it in, and I cannot" (Jeremiah 20:9). My soul would ache if I did not talk about the Lord who saved me. How absurd it would be not to live differently once taken from death to life. How sorrowful it would be not to share life with the spiritually dead around me. By the power of the Holy Spirit, I was driven to give the truth to as many people as I could.

When I shared on Instagram to the few family members and friends who followed along, the goal was never to have tons of followers; it was to help as many people know Him as possible. My focus was not a platform; it was people. My priority was not to gain a large sphere of influence; it was to follow Jesus and lead others to do likewise. Little did I know all the ways I would get to tell people about Him! It really is crazy what God will do through our lives when our hearts are postured in humility with the pure desire to know Him and make Him known.

AN UNASSUMING MOMENT TURNED PIVOTAL

When I was sixteen, I lived in Alabama. I was visiting extended family for Thanksgiving in West Monroe, Louisiana, where my family used to live. One afternoon while there, I met up with some of my childhood friends at a frozen yogurt shop to catch up and just enjoy being with one another. Before we left for a basketball game, we did what most girls love to do when they get together. We took a picture. Sadie Robertson was on my left, Mary Kate Robertson was on my right, and I stood in the middle.

On our way to the basketball game, Sadie shared the picture in a simple, casual Instagram post. Upon getting to the high school gym, Sadie met up with her team and I made my way to the bleachers. As sneakers squeaked along the court and the subtle smell of nacho cheese filled the air, I found my seat. The gym was loud with excitement, and I felt a sweet sense of nostalgia as I got to see family friends I hadn't seen since summer camp. I had so many reasons to smile! While watching the game, I checked my phone and noticed the picture Sadie had posted was getting a lot of attention. And with just one click, my world was rocked. The all-too-familiar desire I had for people to like me was crushed as I read one of the comments: "Who is that ugly girl in the middle?" My heart tightened and felt heavy, like an elephant was standing on it.

In a matter of moments, hundreds of people flooded the comments section with their thoughts about me—the girl in the middle. Crowds of people shared that they didn't like my smile, saying it was cringey and too big. As a sixteen-year-old girl who hoped to get married one day, reading that boys thought I was ugly hurt me deeply. Their comments sent a wave of sadness over me. *Were they typing the words every boy thought about me? Would they have still said these things about me in person, if there weren't a screen between us? Did they forget they were talking about a real person who could see everything they wrote?* The words were brutal and cut like a knife. Their words made me feel like I wasn't enough and like I was too much all at the same time. To them, I wasn't pretty enough, and my joy was way too over the top. How was I supposed to come to terms with that? How could I boldly be my true self while people were saying that they didn't like the way I looked?

Even now, reflecting on that moment, I am asking God to guard my heart as the emotions return. I wish I could go back and hug that girl sitting in the bleachers. I wish I could go back and tell her how beautiful she is, how wonderful her smile is. I wish I could go back, look her in the eyes, and tell her how thankful I am for her, how proud I am to *be* her.

That night, my parents were witnessing the cyberbullying from a few miles down the road at my grandma's house. They saw the comments posted on Sadie's account. They texted me, downright angry that so many people would have the nerve to speak such things about their girl. They asked how I was doing.

In that moment, sitting in the bleachers, I found myself in the middle of two options. I could sulk in fear of what everyone thought. I could come into agreement with the cruel comments and join them in critiquing my own smile. I could conform to who I thought the bullies wanted me to be and try to fit the mold they thought would be attractive. I could grow timid and stop smiling so much so I wouldn't run the risk of being bullied again.

. . . Or . . .

I could think on "Whatever is true, whatever is honorable, whatever is just, whatever is pure, whatever is lovely, whatever is commendable, if there is any excellence, if there is anything worthy of praise" (Philippians 4:8). I could stand firm on the truth I had come to know about who my God is and who I am in Christ. I could keep smiling with confidence because I was unashamed of the joy God had undeniably given me. I could stand on the truth that this joy I carried was not cringey or too much; rather it was a testament to the holy God alive inside of me. I could pray for God to be glorified through the horrible circumstance I found myself in the middle of as I sat in the bleachers. And I could pray for the very people who found it necessary to let me know they thought I was ugly.

The first option seemed to be the easiest. Shrinking back seemed like a choice that was offered as low-hanging fruit, to be grasped with almost no effort. My feelings were hurt and so many of my thoughts were steeped in insecurity. To join in with the critiquing and become timid in my own skin wouldn't have been all that difficult. So, yes, the first option would have been easier in the moment, but easiest doesn't always mean best.

As I sat there, I navigated all the thoughts and feelings that filled my heart and mind. I experienced what seemed like a tangible dichotomy. While there was a pang in my stomach from the sickening words people spewed, I was also fully aware of a peace and calmness that was clearly guarding my heart and mind (Philippians 4:7). I felt the protection of God's Word surrounding me. The scripture I had filled myself with for years leading up to this moment was being brought back to my full attention.

Psalm 91 says that God "will command his angels concerning you to guard you in all your ways. On their hands they will bear you up, lest you strike your foot against a stone" (Psalm 91:11–12, NIV). I was still in the moment, but at the same time, I was lifted above my circumstances and given eyes to see God was doing something bigger. His angels ministered to me (Hebrews 1:14) amid the scoreboard buzzing and mean comments pinging. In that brief period that felt like an eternity, God reminded me that my battle was not against the bullies. As I sat in the bleachers that night, my battle was "against the rulers, against the authorities, against the powers of this dark world and against the spiritual forces of evil in the heavenly realms" (Ephesians 6:12, NIV). There was more happening than met the human eye. While the words of people were so harsh, God's words of authority met me and secured me as I pondered in such a deep space of vulnerability. The social media opinions coming in one after another were chaotically loud, but God's still, small voice is the sound I heard most distinctly. God's words were more powerful than the words of people—I was personally experiencing this in real time. Amid processing so many feelings and thoughts, God brought to my mind a quote I had written on a notecard and taped to my bedroom wall: "I am a daughter of the King, who is not moved by the world. For my God is with me and goes before me. I do not fear because I am His." I responded to my parents' text with this quote, fully confident in every single word.

I don't mean to make it sound like I was impervious to the pain of criticism. Fear was on the scene. Insecurity made an impressive effort to take up great capacity in my mind. But rather than directing my response, these real emotions gave me more reasons to cling to God. My struggles reminded me of how much I needed His guidance, His counsel, and His peace. I was discovering firsthand that there is great strength found when we take all that we are feeling to the Lord and trust Him as we walk with Him in the middle of it all.

This is what Paul must have meant when he wrote to the church in Corinth, "Christ's love compels us" (2 Corinthians 5:14, NIV). In my own strength, I could not move forward with boldness and joy. My own willpower was not enough to give me the endurance I needed that night. Christ's love, on the other hand, was more than enough. Dwelling on His love for me gave me a soul at rest, and reflecting on His love toward me drove me to extend that same love to others—even the people who hated and berated me. The love of Christ changed my perspective. The love of Christ called me out of my comfort zone. The love of Christ compelled me to respond differently—to respond in a way that was not focused on myself, but rather on Him who died, was buried, and rose again for me, and for them.

After the basketball game, Sadie gave me a ride back to my grandma's house. She had not yet seen the spiral of cyberbullying that had taken over the comments section of her post, as she had been playing basketball when it all went down.

Not too long into our drive Sadie asked, "Emma, what do you do when people misunderstand your joy?" I looked at her, thinking about how ironic and timely it was for her to ask such a question.

I said, "You know, it's funny that you ask, because there are a lot of people misunderstanding my joy right now." Explaining the situation that had unfolded in the bleachers, I told her that the people who weren't loving me well probably didn't know how much God loved them. "We never know what people are going through," I said. "What a great opportunity this is to love people!" I knew that if my confidence wasn't in what people thought, my confidence couldn't be taken away when people thought poorly of me.

Jesus said, "If the world hates you, know that it has hated me before it hated you. If you were of the world, the world would love you as its own; but because you are not of the world, but I chose you out of the world, therefore the world hates you" (John 15:18–19). We don't need to be surprised when the world tells us to calm down and mocks proudly as it does so. Jesus already warned us that many would respond to us in this way. These words of Jesus challenged me that night to keep letting my light shine even when my feelings were hurt (Matthew 5:16). They also comforted me with the knowledge that Jesus deeply understood what I was going through. He was not only Lord over my situation, He also empathized with me in the middle of it.

He was not only Lord over my situation, He also empathized with me in the middle of it.

Later that night, though I was trying to stay away from Sadie's post, the comments felt like they were screaming through the phone. Curiosity tugged at me. I just wanted to know what one more person was saying, even if knowing would set me up for a spiral of discouragement. Putting my phone down and choosing not to read what people wrote was often harder for me to do than I would like to admit. In frequent moments of weakness, I needed the help of my closest people and the Holy Spirit to continually set my gaze on Jesus rather than on the opinions of people. Fixing my thoughts on the thoughts of strangers was only stirring up anxiety and giving fear room to take root in me.

COMPELLED BY LOVE

Confidence in God was, and still is, a moment-by-moment journey. Trusting in God was not a one-time decision I made at age fourteen, when I surrendered to Christ as my Lord and Savior. Living by faith is an everyday, step-by-step walk with God. And when we set our hearts on Him, His comfort brings us joy when anxiety is great within us, and His presence encourages us to not fear because He is our God (Psalm 94:19; Isaiah 41:10, NIV).

> Living by faith is an everyday, step-by-step
> walk with God.

When I had woken up on that dreary November morning, I didn't know all that would take place in that day. But God did. He knew all that was coming and was faithful to carry me in His arms from the moment I woke up, to the moment I sat in the bleachers, to the moment I laid my head on my pillow that night (Psalm 68:19). God is the one who made the difference in my ability to respond boldly in love. Remembering God's faithfulness and recalling His promises strengthened me in the fullness of joy (Psalm 16:11). The Bible says in 2 Timothy 3:16–17 that the Word of God thoroughly equips us for every good work. That day, I witnessed how His Word gave me all that I needed to trust Him even when it was hard. I experienced how His Word spurred me on in zeal to keep following Him with my whole heart.

When I woke up the next morning, I found out that thousands of people had made their way to my Instagram account. Coming to see more about "the girl in the middle," they found more about Jesus. Whether they were coming to my account for encouragement, whether they were coming out of curiosity as to what all the talk was about, or whether they were coming to get a good laugh and make fun of me, it didn't matter. They were coming! And I kept sharing. I kept sharing because sharing mattered more than the ridicule that could come from it.

If we were to look at any sports team, we would find that they have put in hours upon hours of practice. They schedule time for early workouts, they put intentional meal plans in place to meet nutrition goals, and they prioritize late-night studying of film to prepare for the competition against their next opponent. Why is this? Why are they putting in so much time and effort day in and day out?

Because they want to win.

The team works so diligently and stewards their time as they do because they are driven by a desire to be champions. In other words, they are compelled by a longing to be the best.

We are all compelled by something. We all have a reason why we live life the way we do. The way we go about our days, make our decisions, and leverage our time reflects what compels us. For some of us, status and success in our career urges us to revolve our lives around our job. For others of us, the need to be liked inspires us to live in a way we think others will approve of. And there are those of us who are motivated by the need for control and, therefore, live a life filled with worry as each day greets us with unknowns.

The thing that compels us determines the kind of life we live. When the apostle Paul wrote in 2 Corinthians 5:14 (NIV), "For Christ's love compels us," he was saying that he and those in ministry with him were so radically transformed by the love of Jesus that they were left with no other option but for their lives to be entirely motivated by this love. Paul was completely captivated by the gospel, and therefore he made decisions and spent his time in a way that reflected that. The most fitting response when we experience the love of Christ is to take action in bold faith, driven to make the most of every opportunity we have to share Him, and to live with a sense of urgency about the things of heaven. When we are compelled by the love of Christ, we don't live for ourselves anymore. We live for Him and make the decision to submit to His Word, to His ways. When we are compelled by His love, we are confident in the love He has for us and are on a committed mission of spreading His love to the world—even to those who are cruel to us for doing so. When the love of Christ compels us, we start prioritizing what He has spoken over what people feel the need to comment. When we live compelled by His love, we move forward in a purpose bigger than ourselves.

WE ALL STAND IN THE MIDDLE

Being a Christian is about much more than having a Bible verse in our Instagram bio. To know God is more than going to a Christian school when we are young. Living out our faith is more than sitting in a pew on a Sunday morning. While those things are great, we're missing the point of Christianity if that's all we think it boils down to. We are missing what really matters if we don't have a personal love for God and a life that is unashamedly devoted to Him.

In *Knowing God,* J. I. Packer wrote that "knowing [God] involves going with him."[1] In other words, knowing God is not merely something we say we are doing. The proof of knowing God is a life lived with Him and like Him. If we aren't closely walking with Him each day, then we will lack the zeal and steadfastness to boldly live out our faith day by day.

The Cultural Research Center at Arizona Christian University recently completed a study that revealed "a full 69% of U.S. adults self-identify as Christian [but] in reality only a tiny minority of American adults (6%) possess a biblical worldview and demonstrate a consistent understanding and application of biblical principles."[2] This is where many of us find ourselves today, claiming to be Christian but neglecting to actually live like it. We are lacking a biblical worldview because we aren't going to God's Word for direction in our lives. And because we lack a biblical worldview, it makes sense that we aren't living in accordance with what the Word says. Our fears and our desire for instant gratification are driving our lives instead of love for God, causing us to self-identify with the title "Christian" but not actually embrace the essence of what it means to be one.

Being a Christian is not a surface-level title to merely claim with our lips, but a heart-level life to carry out with our actions.

The director of research at the Cultural Research Center, George Barna, says, " 'Christian' has become somewhat of a generic term rather than a name that reflects deep commitment to passionately pursuing and being like Jesus Christ."[3] This exposes the reality that many of us claim with our mouths to follow Jesus, but in our hearts we are far from Him (Matthew 15:8). Being a Christian is not a surface-level title to merely claim with our lips, but a heart-level life to carry out with our actions.

Your decision to boldly live out your faith in Jesus is not going to come from whether you have attached yourself to the label of Christianity. Your choice will overflow from your personal closeness with Him, your trust in Him, and your diligence of hiding His Word in your heart. It is going to come from your desire to walk with Him more than you want anything else. It is going to come from His love being what compels your life.

The life-changing moment for me in my experience from high school was not the moment that everyone saw online. It was not me standing between two of my dear friends in front of a frozen yogurt shop. It wasn't the photograph. It wasn't even the post and all the comments. No, the pivotal moment was something very few people even noticed as it happened. It took place as I sat in the bleachers watching the cruel comments flood in. *In that sacred space, I had the choice to live compelled by the love of Christ . . . or by the world.* In the two years prior, while hiding God's Word in my heart, He had been preparing me not only for that moment in the bleachers but also for a million moments to follow, as the bullying for my faith and how I looked would continue for years to come.

That moment in the bleachers was what I like to call a "middle moment." Middle moments are the instances where we find ourselves standing in the middle of a choice to make—either we boldly live out our faith in Jesus or we let our desire to stay comfortable make the call. It is when we are faced with an opportunity to either go with God or take the path of least resistance. Middle moments are not a new concept, either.

In Jeremiah 6:16 (NIV), the Lord said to His people, "Stand at the crossroads and look; ask for the ancient paths, ask where the good way is, and walk in it, and you will find rest for your souls." God was calling the Israelites' attention to the decision that lay before them—the decision to either walk along the path of His commandments or along the path of their own way. He sincerely desired for them to come to Him, to seek out the truth He gave them long ago in the wilderness through His servant, Moses. Not only did He long to show them the good way, but He also longed for them to experience rest for their souls.

We too stand at a crossroads. We not only stand at a crossroads when considering whether we will put our trust in Jesus Christ as the Lord and Savior of our life, but we stand there every single day thereafter as we walk in relationship with Him as His disciple. When I sat in the bleachers on that November night, I sat at a crossroads. When we run into someone in town who is hard to get along with, we stand at a crossroads. When we see that the Lord is leading us to go in a direction that is not in alignment with our own five-year plan, we stand at a crossroads. We stand at the crossroads in our homes, on our campuses, and in our workplaces as we are met with opportunities to live compelled by the love of Christ.

These crossroads are middle moments, where we have the daily choice of either doing what makes us feel the most comfortable, or asking God for guidance—and, by the power of His Spirit, living out what He says. We all have room to grow in this. We all need the Holy Spirit to become more like Jesus, and boldly live out our faith each day. This is not a book about pulling ourselves up by the bootstraps and practicing our faith by our own means and willpower, out of strife. No, Paul wrote that "it is God who works in you, both to will and to work for his good pleasure" (Philippians 2:13). C. S. Lewis expressed, "After the first few steps in the Christian life we realize that everything which really needs to be done in our souls can only be done by God."[4] Together, we are going to draw near to God and, through Him, actually live out what it means to be His follower.

Before any change is made in our lives, though, we must first do what God called the Israelites to do. We must first stand, look, and recognize that change is needed. God is beckoning us to be aware of and confess the daily moments in which we are choosing our comfort over His ancient, good paths. God is so kind that He not only wants to give us eyes to see our middle moments, but He also wants to personally, closely show us the best choices to make. God wants us to live driven by His love, no matter what, because He knows that living that kind of life satisfies our souls like nothing and no one else can.

The words etched onto these pages are to show you that you too are the girl in the middle, standing at the crossroads each day with an incredible opportunity before you. Every day you too sit in your own set of bleachers with the chance to boldly live as a follower of Jesus Christ—or not. You are the girl in the middle, given a daily choice to live compelled by comfort or compelled by the love of God.

You are the girl in the middle, given a
daily choice to live compelled by comfort
or compelled by the love of God.

In the chapters that follow, we are going to do what the Lord asked of His people so many years ago. We will first look at where we are, acknowledging that we are daily at a crossroads, presented with the choice to go with Him or not. We are going to identify the things that have been compelling our lives instead of Christ's love. We are going to expose the ways of our flesh and the tactics of the evil one that have been holding us back from boldly living out our faith in Jesus Christ. We are going to discover what living compelled by the love of Christ looks like and how we can do that in our own lives. Lastly, we are going to dive into what happens on the other side of our middle moments, on the other side of choosing Christ at our daily crossroads. We will unpack the Scriptures to discover how we can best navigate the things that are bound to come with taking the good, ancient paths. I pray that as you read these pages, you may be led by the Spirit to "understand what really matters, so that you may live pure and blameless lives until the day of Christ's return" (Philippians 1:10, NLT). Doing so will not be perfect, predictable, or easy. Rather it will be a difficult, trying, countercultural journey. Guaranteed, though, it will be a beautiful one that is worth your time, effort, and any sacrifice you will make. This journey is worth your whole life!

You were made for this. You were made to walk with God, step by step, in the purposeful life He gave you. You were made a masterpiece in Christ Jesus to do good things that God planned long ago for you to do (Ephesians 2:10, NLT). You were made, not just to be loved by God, but to live from His love, courageously expressing your faith through the life you live (2 Corinthians 5:14, NIV). Fear's time of calling the shots is gone. Letting your love for comfort override your love for God has had its hour. Attaching yourself to the label of Christianity while not living it out is over. The right time to live the life you were made for is right now.

Let's journey together. Let's go all in.

2

Change of Perspective

We don't see things as they are. We see them as we are.

—ANAÏS NIN

In 1296 the Republic of Florence founded the Opera del Duomo, a council of officials responsible for overseeing construction of a new cathedral, the Santa Maria del Fiore. In 1408 the council had the idea of placing twelve grand statues along the roofline of the cathedral. After considering who could take on the task of sculpting the third statue, in 1464 they commissioned a man named Agostino di Duccio. Di Duccio went to Carrara, Italy, to select the slab of marble for the project, rightfully so as this place "has long been known as the Italian capital of marble."[1] The twelve-thousand-pound slab of marble Di Duccio selected was carved and shipped to Florence for the project. Unfortunately, it was in pretty rough condition. The marble was rather narrow, had small holes, and had veins that could be seen throughout. The difficulty of sculpting with this chosen stone was probably akin to a painter being given a dingy canvas covered with scratches—not the easiest start to such a grand project.

Soon after receiving the great piece of marble, Di Duccio was unable to find use for the stone and he gave up. The forsaken marble collected dust. In 1475, a full ten years later, a man named Antonio Rossellino stepped in to see what he could do. But he too became convinced that the marble slab was too hard to work with, so he called it quits pretty quickly. Twenty-five years later, that marble block, declared unusable and neglected by not one but two artists, remained in the courtyard of the cathedral.

About thirty-five years passed before the cathedral council sought once again to consider the massive project. They were approached by an eager young artist in 1501 and decided to let him take on the challenge. Greeting the incredibly flawed, weathered, rejected slab, this twenty-six-year-old sculptor chiseled away at the stone in secrecy for almost three years. Not only was he carving into an imperfect, ginormous piece of marble, but he also was working with the incomplete attempts left behind from the previous sculptors. This added to the strenuous work before him.

In 1504 the statue was complete and ready to be revealed. As the council witnessed the seventeen-foot-tall work of art, they were utterly amazed. They were finally seeing their vision for the cathedral come to life. Rather than placing the beautiful statue on the roof of the cathedral, as originally intended, they displayed it outside of the city hall in Florence because it was too big to put in its initially intended place, and because the council wanted it to be enjoyed by all the people. The statue of David, also known as The Giant, "has become one of the most recognizable statues in the entire world of art," being visited by more than a million people a year and still inspiring artists to this day.[2] Its carver was the one and only Michelangelo.

Michelangelo stood before the same marble slab that Di Duccio and Rossellino faced. He saw all the flaws they saw and more, because of the years of weather damage and incomplete work caused by its abandonment. All three sculptors were given the same task. So what was the difference? How did Michelangelo create such beauty when the others didn't even find the slab of marble usable? Why would he sign up for the challenge, endure for almost three years to see it through, and—as historians share—even be eager to do so?

I am convinced that his willingness, eagerness, and endurance was possible because of the way he saw the task. I believe he saw the masterpiece hidden within the flawed slab *before* it was actually carved out to see and touch. What the other artists saw as six tons of stone that was too far gone, Michelangelo saw as an opportunity to create something magnificent.

Michelangelo found himself in the middle of a decision. He could easily have backed out. It is probable that no one would have blamed him for passing on this project.

Not only did Michelangelo's pure enjoyment of sculpting shape his consideration of the task at hand, but his preparation also gave him eyes to see the challenge as one he could definitely conquer. For half his life he had been preparing to create such a masterpiece. He had been under the apprenticeship of the painter Domenico Ghirlandaio. He had studied classical sculpture in the palace of the Medici family. He had gained knowledge on cadavers which taught him a great deal of anatomy. He was taught literature and sculpture technique in Bologna and Venice, and all of this took place before he even started officially working as a sculptor! He was ready for this challenge, and recalling the investment he had made leading up to that moment gave him eyes to see this vision come to life. So he started and finished what came to be known as one of his greatest works—and one of the greatest works the world has ever seen. Yes, Michelangelo was an incredible sculptor, and yes, this was a tall order, but it was his view of the challenge that directly affected how he navigated it—and in turn, changed history.

Just as with Michelangelo, the way we look at the challenges before us matters. We could be the most well-prepared and fit person to claim the feat, and still cower down in fear. Not because of the hardship itself, but because of the lens we are seeing it through.

SEEING THE SAME CHALLENGE DIFFERENTLY

In the Bible, there's a group of men who also found themselves up against an "intimidating slab of marble," if you will, and were met with the choice of how they would view the challenge. The Israelites had the Promised Land in sight, and the time was finally approaching to leave the wilderness and step into what God had prepared for them. This was the land that God had promised to Abraham, Isaac, and Jacob. At the burning bush, God told Moses he would faithfully deliver his people into this land. Years upon years of promises had led up to this moment that they were now standing in. The leader of the Israelites, Moses, commissioned twelve spies to scope out the land. He instructed them to take note of everything and to bring back a report on all they saw.

Upon arriving in Canaan, the twelve spies observed the land and all that filled it. For forty days they studied the stature of the giants as they walked the streets. They gazed up and noted the height of the city's fortified walls. They had time to form a solid view of the land as they analyzed it in secret.

What were their conversations with each other like while taking in all that they saw? What thoughts were running through their minds as they lay down to rest in the evenings? What did they talk about with one another on their way back after the long weeks away? Were their conversations consumed with all the possibilities of what could go wrong if they were to try to conquer the land? Or were they meditating on all that God had promised in the years leading up to this moment, amazed that they were given such a special role in the fulfillment of His long-awaited word? How they chose to respond after seeing everything the land entailed would expose their true perspective not just of the task before them, but of God Himself.

When the spies came back, the entire nation gathered to hear their report. Ten of the twelve spies delivered their news, terrified. They spoke fearfully about how the Canaanites were stronger than they were, that their land was very large, and that there was no way they could stand a chance against them. They even went on to say that, compared to the giants who lived there, they themselves looked like grasshoppers. This detail seems to unveil what thoughts ruminated in their minds. As this negative report was being shared and spread, fear began to take over the crowd of Israelites to the point that the whole nation was in shambles.

One of the other two spies who had not yet shared his recap of the trip, Caleb, told everyone to stop the nonsense. He said, "Let us go up at once and occupy it, for we are well able to overcome it" (Numbers 13:30). While it would have been lovely for the whole nation to snap out of it and take a deep breath of relief at Caleb's words, they completely disagreed with him. They proceeded to cry all night long, even thinking it would be better if they went back to Egypt where they had been slaves!

While the Israelites continued complaining, Caleb and another spy named Joshua tore their clothes to show their deep grief over the nation's lack of trust in God. They boldly started telling the whole crowd that because God was with them, they didn't need to be afraid. But the nation was in such an uproar and so consumed with resistance to going anywhere near the Promised Land that they became outraged with the two spies.

Joshua and Caleb had seen the same land and the same giants the other ten spies had seen, and yet they were confident that they could prevail. Why was there such a substantial difference in how these men responded in this middle moment?

RESPONDING TO FEAR

How we look at a situation plays a significant role in our response to it. Our perspective is the difference between living out of fear and moving forward in courage even when fear is still present. To be clear, fear is not an emotion to despise. Often, we think of fear as a bad thing entirely, but it is incredibly important to note that in many ways, fear demonstrates how thoughtful God was when He made us. He put an awareness of danger in us to protect us. Fear is what keeps us from running across the street without looking or walking down a dark alley at night by ourselves. There is a healthiness about fear that keeps us alive, gives us common sense, and helps us remain alert when necessary.

God literally wired our brains to help us stay protected and be on guard for danger by giving us the amygdala. The amygdala in our brain is quite small (about the size of an almond) but has a pretty big job. Aside from many other important functions such as our memory and learning abilities, the amygdala is significant when it comes to helping us regulate our emotions, including the emotion of fear. When we feel like we are in danger, this small part of our brain sends signals to the hypothalamus, which then gets the sympathetic nervous system going. The sympathetic nerves send messages to the adrenal glands and our body fills with adrenaline. This leads to the feelings we know all too well, such as the sweaty palms and racing heartbeat that show up when we're afraid or super nervous.[3]

This whole process that the amygdala kicks off happens in "less than 100 milliseconds, just one-tenth of a second. . . . [But] should the terror prove benign, you'll not long be in fear's thrall."[4] This means that once we realize whatever we are facing is harmless, we tend to feel the freedom to relax again.

The fear that the Israelites experienced was entirely normal. It was a part of being human. They were not wrong for being afraid. I bet all twelve spies had racing hearts, clammy hands, and a tightened chest when they saw the giants they were supposed to stand up against walking around the land. It makes total sense that the amygdala would have been sending red flags to let them know they needed protection. I can just imagine the amount of adrenaline rushing through their bloodstream, seeing how fortified the cities were. Their walk through Canaan was no walk in the park. The difference between the spies was probably not that some felt fear and others didn't. The difference was definitely not that some were in an intimidating circumstance and others weren't. The difference was that ten spies were still in fear's thrall, while Caleb and Joshua knew the terror to be benign because they knew God was with them.

Their perspective made the difference. Caleb and Joshua were not held in fear's thrall as the others were, because God's promises shaped their perspective and because they trusted Him. Just as Michelangelo had years of preparation behind him that helped him have the right perspective to take on his challenge, so did Caleb and Joshua have years of preparation that equipped them for that moment. Their preparation might not have looked like years of schooling, but it did look like witnessing God deliver them from slavery in Egypt. It looked like walking on dry ground because God had parted the Red Sea for them. Their point of view was shaped by eating manna from heaven and drinking water from a rock. God had led them by a cloud in the day and by a pillar of fire at night. He had promised that He would bring them to the Promised Land. Their knowledge of God, their remembrance of His Word, and their recollection of what He had done fueled their faith in Him. They believed that God was their provider, protector, and promise keeper. Because they remembered God's faithfulness, they trusted Him to be faithful again. Their years of experiencing God's authority and care prepared them to not let fear determine their response in this middle moment facing the giants. They were empowered with confidence even in the face of such a scary circumstance.

The other ten spies were just as prepared as Joshua and Caleb. Just as Di Duccio and Rossellino looked at the same challenging marble block as Michelangelo, the other ten spies stood in front of the same set of giants Joshua and Caleb did. Not only that, but they had also witnessed God's miracles in the years prior, just as Joshua and Caleb had. The difference was that the ten spies saw the terror of the giants and chose to forget God had already conquered all the terrors of their past. They cowered, captured in fear's thrall because God's faithfulness did not determine their perspective. The ten spies were fully equipped to step up to the challenge by God's power, but they didn't have eyes to see that they could do it because they didn't see God for who He was. Their perspective of God determined how they dealt with the fear they felt. Because their perspective of Him was inaccurate, fear was calling the shots.

WHO DO YOU SAY THAT I AM?

What would it look like for our day-to-day fears to be proven benign? What would it take for us to relax when faced with the loss of control that comes with stepping into the unknown? What would allow us to remain at ease when people don't like us for our faith in Jesus? What would cause us to no longer buckle under the fear of suffering in our walk with Jesus? Will the things that terrify us in our walk with God no longer bind us if they never happen? Or is it possible to live free from fear's thrall even if the very thing we are afraid of happens? What if our fears became "benign" not because the scary situations and uncomfortable circumstances in life went away, but because our perspective shifted?

Our perspective of God directly impacts our perspective of the circumstances we face. A. W. Tozer wrote, "What comes into our minds when we think about God is the most important thing about us."[5] We can find freedom from fear's thrall, not by the objects of our fear disappearing, but by our perspective of God being fine-tuned. Our perspective of God matters. What we believe to be true about God doesn't change who He is, but it changes everything about who we are and how we live. Who we believe Him to be and what we believe Him to be like directly impacts the perspective we have of ourselves, our relationships, and the situations we face every day. Because many of us have an inaccurate perspective of God, we are living compelled by fear rather than living compelled by His love.

What we believe to be true about God doesn't change who He is, but it changes everything about who we are and how we live.

Our perspective of God has been shaped with complexity over the course of our entire life, whether we have been aware of it or not. Multiple factors weigh in, contributing to who we believe God to be and what we believe Him to be like. The people we listen to play a major role in how we view God, and therefore how we view our own lives. If we are going to start living compelled by the love of Christ, we must start with addressing who we even see Christ to be. One of the ways we can get clarity on our own view of Christ is by evaluating our beliefs about what others say is true about Him, such as when Jesus asked his disciples:

> "Who do people say that the Son of Man is?" And they said, "Some say John the Baptist, others say Elijah, and others Jeremiah or one of the prophets." He said to them, "But who do you say that I am?" Simon Peter replied, "You are the Christ, the Son of the living God." (Matthew 16:13–16)

Just as people were voicing their opinions thousands of years ago about who they thought the Son of Man to be, people are continuing to voice their opinions today. Like the disciples, we too could spout off what we have heard many people say about Jesus. In our world today we can hear a variety of views with the simple click of a button. We can go on social media and hear one hundred different perspectives in a matter of a few minutes spent scrolling. Millions of sermons are at our disposal. Podcasts, the news, and social media deliver ideas and quotes and messages left and right. And not to mention our own schools and workplaces and homes are filled with different points of view on who God is and what He is like. If our perspective of God directly impacts the life we live, it is worth our due diligence to take note of the voices we are giving attention to.

Beyond just wanting the disciples to be aware of what they heard others say about Him, Jesus got personal with them. He wanted to hear their own perspectives. There is a difference between answering for the crowds and answering for ourselves. Our familiarity with many opinions is not the same thing as having clarity on what we personally believe. If we settle into thinking that the collective perspective around us is automatically our own, then we will fail to seek understanding about why we have the point of view we do. I wonder how many of the Israelites would have gone with Joshua and Caleb had they not so quickly believed that the ten spies were correct. What difference would it have made had they paused, stepped away from the majority, considered all God had done, and sincerely reflected on what their own perspective of God was? Would they have trusted God even though it went against the majority?

The experiences we have journeyed through in life also significantly influence our perspective of God. Though the Israelites had experienced years of seeing God perform signs and wonders, providing for them daily, and faithfully leading them as He promised, they also had experienced years of brutal oppression from the Egyptians. They had probably grown so weary of such a drawn-out hardship that they doubted if God even heard them. Maybe they began to question God's love for them. On top of all that, they were saturated with pagan ideologies, witnessing the

Egyptians prosper as they worshipped their many gods day after day. It is likely that they wondered if their God was worth relying on, whether He was the only true God. When hearing from the ten spies how tall the giants stood and how fortified the cities of the Promised Land were, the Israelites didn't respond from all the times they saw God's faithfulness. They responded from years of experiencing hardship that cultivated in them a lack of trust in God. They responded from the experiences that they had allowed to negatively shape their perspective.

In the same way, we have experienced hurt from leaders in our churches. We have seen people who claim to be Christian live an entirely unchristian lifestyle. Many of us have grown up in homes where maybe we prayed for healing and restoration, but now divorce, abuse, and illness are some of the engraved memories from our childhood. And not only do we toss and turn over these struggles in our own lives, but our souls ache as we look at the turmoil those around the world are experiencing as well. This is all so real, and whether we have realized it or not, this has all affected the way we see God, and who we believe Him to be.

When we are aware of the many layers that have piled up and given shape to our perspective of God throughout our life, what do we do with it all? How do we discern between the truth and the lies we are believing about God? If living compelled by the love of Christ requires seeing Christ rightly, how do we start seeing Him for who He is?

Someone in Scripture who taught us how to find clarity in our foggy perspective of God was a man named Asaph. In Psalm 73 he vulnerably expressed that, like us, the voices he heard and the tough experiences he suffered brought a tension in his soul regarding what he should think about God. He shared how easy it felt to doubt the Lord. Like the Israelites in the wilderness, he might have seen God's goodness before, but he was tempted to question it because of the circumstance he was currently in. Then, after sharing so many raw emotions and thoughts, he pondered what to do with it all, what to do with his confused view of God. Failing to find clear perspective on his own, he concluded to take his struggle, his contradicting thoughts, and his frustrations to the Lord. He said, "But when I thought how to understand this, it seemed to me a wearisome task, until I went into the sanctuary of God; then I discerned" (Psalm 73:16–17). He chose to go to God with his questions and unrest. He went to God to find a perspective established on truth. He confessed that trying to know God better on his own was wearisome, but when he chose to go to God to learn what God's heart was like, he found discernment, he found a changed perspective.

Filtering and processing through the many voices we hear and all the experiences we have walked through takes help. As Asaph showed, we cannot discover an accurate perspective of God by ourselves. We need God's help to see Him rightly, and thankfully, He invites us to personally come to Him with all our questions, doubts, and blind spots. We go to Him by submitting to His Word, by talking with Him in prayer, and by having godly community around us to sort through all that currently makes up our perspective of God. Just as Jesus wanted to personally hear how the disciples saw Him, He wants to hear how you and I see Him too. When we humble ourselves and seek Him, we are promised to find Him, promised to see Him more for who He is (Matthew 7:7–8). After Peter declared Jesus to be the Son of God, Jesus told him that he was blessed because "flesh and blood has not revealed this to you, but My Father who is in heaven" (Matthew 16:17). God Himself revealed who He was to Peter, and God is still revealing Himself to you and me today.

> When we humble ourselves and seek Him,
> we are promised to find Him, promised to
> see Him more for who He is.

After going to God and finding understanding, Asaph wrote:

Then I realized that my heart was bitter, and I was all torn up inside. I was foolish and ignorant—I must have seemed like a senseless animal to you. Yet I still belong to you; you hold my right hand. You guide me with your counsel, leading me to a glorious destiny. (Psalm 73:21–24, NLT)

When we choose to seek the Lord, He is kind to teach us, correct us, rebuke us, and train us in what is right (2 Timothy 3:16, NIV). He shows us our own heart and reveals to us where the lies we believe about Him came from. He puts a mirror in front of our hearts so that we might clearly see ourselves in the light of who He is. Asaph was humbled by the amazing reality that even in his skewed perspective of God, God still faithfully led him and helped him learn to see through the lens of truth. We can look at this and be encouraged that the Lord is not turned away by our misunderstanding or inaccurate perspective of Him. Even when our eyes are clouded with bitterness and ignorance, making it hard to trust Him, He is right there, wanting us to come to Him honestly. With overwhelming grace, He delights in showing us who He really is, which in turn equips us to trust Him and no longer be in fear's thrall.

3

Excuses

He that is good for making excuses is seldom good for anything else.

—BENJAMIN FRANKLIN

I once read a poem by Shel Silverstein about a little girl named Peggy Ann McKay expressing why she couldn't go to school. After listing off reason after reason she couldn't attend, she finds out that it happens to be Saturday. With great joy, she says, "G'bye, I'm going out to play!"[1] All of her sicknesses and discomforts magically disappear the moment she discovers school is not in session. This led me to think about how as kids we would look for any excuse as to why we had to miss school or were unable to eat our vegetables or couldn't turn in our homework. Though this seems lighthearted and quite silly, the heart of this tendency grows up with us. As adults we let the clean basket of laundry sit unfolded for days on end because we are too tired to tend to it. When we are late to work, it seems to regularly be because of traffic. We don't work out anymore because we just don't have the time. And these are small examples.

In the face of a challenge, excuses keep us from stepping up to the plate and getting things done. In the face of a mistake, excuses keep us from admitting that we messed up. They keep us from growing. Disguising themselves as a safety net, excuses only keep us comfortable and hold us back from truly living.

One of the ways our perspective reveals itself is through the excuses we make in response to God's daily call in our lives. Excuses have a way of getting in the way. They get in the way of our trust in God. They get in the way of our obedience to Him. Whether we think we are too old, too young, too inexperienced, too weak, too introverted, or too far gone, we let these insecurities hold us back from boldly living out our faith. We seem to live convinced that our inadequacies are too big for God. Many of us are living compelled by excuses in our middle moments rather than by the love of Christ.

"WHO AM I?"

Moses was a Hebrew by birth but raised by Egyptians. The Israelites, God's chosen people, were being oppressed with harsh labor by the Egyptians while Moses was growing into his adulthood. When Moses was around forty, Scripture says:

He went out to his people and looked on their burdens, and he saw an Egyptian beating a Hebrew, one of his people. He looked this way and that, and seeing no one, he struck down the Egyptian and hid him in the sand. (Exodus 2:11–12)

It didn't take long for Pharaoh, the king of Egypt, to find out about it, and he wanted Moses killed for what he had done. Scared for his life, Moses fled to a town called Midian and started a new life there. He got married, had children, and was a shepherd for his father-in-law's flock. This in and of itself was a significant indicator that Moses was leaving his Egyptian upbringing behind, because the job of shepherding was considered the lowliest of the lowly by the Egyptians. Well acquainted with his new day-to-day, Moses lived in Midian for forty years.

Now eighty, Moses was living a life his younger self probably never imagined. While out with the sheep one day at Horeb, called the mountain of God, Moses caught sight of a bush that was burning yet not wilting (Exodus 3:1–2). Curiosity consumed him to the point that he had to go investigate, but little did he know that he was stepping toward a monumental moment in history.

This is often how monumental moments in our own lives go. It is the mundane, unassuming moments that hold the possibility of immense life change, incredible growth, and impact that goes beyond what we could have ever expected. The reason these moments hold possibility and not assurance is because we do have a part to play. Will we overlook them or be distracted from giving our attention to them? Or, like Moses, will we lean in with curiosity and find the significance that they hold—the significance that God delights in showing us and invites us to participate in?

It is the mundane, unassuming moments that
hold the possibility of immense life change,
incredible growth, and impact that goes
beyond what we could have ever expected.

God took note of Moses's intrigue and called him by name saying, "Moses, Moses!" (Exodus 3:4). Commentator Douglas Stuart wrote:

> In ancient Semitic culture, addressing someone by saying his or her name twice was a way of expressing endearment, that is, affection and friendship. Thus Moses would have understood immediately that he was being addressed by someone who loved him and was concerned about him.[2]

God was personal with Moses and spoke from a place of so much care toward him. Already, we are seeing God debunk the excuses that the enemy so badly wants us to believe. Believing that our age disqualifies God's capacity to use us fully is quite easy. We tend to think that the season of life we are in puts us in a box and limits God's ability to work in and through our lives, but here we see God personally calling an eighty-year-old man by name for a purpose. Neither our age nor our current stage in life has the power to override God's plan for our lives. In fact, He is the kind of God who intentionally works in and through the very season we are in to bring great glory to His name.

Hearing God call him by name with great endearment, Moses said, "Here I am" (Exodus 3:4). God proceeded to tell Moses not to come any closer and to take off his sandals because the place he stood was holy ground. The ground was not holy because of the land itself. The ground was not holy because Moses was standing on it. No, it was holy because the very presence of God was on that ground. Moses took off his sandals, and God introduced Himself saying, "I am the God of your father, the God of Abraham, the God of Isaac, and the God of Jacob" (Exodus 3:6). He then started explaining to Moses that He had seen the affliction of His people, He had heard their cries while being enslaved by the Egyptians, and He knew their sufferings. He told Moses that He Himself was coming down to deliver them from their bondage and into the land He had for them.

Notice that before God told Moses to do anything, say anything, or go anywhere, He showed him who He was. He showed Moses His heart. Before God did anything, He pointed to Himself, revealing that He was the Lord who had been faithful in every generation past and cared about His people. Prior to God giving Moses any assignment, he wanted Moses to know that God was going to deliver the Israelites. He wanted to ensure that Moses's attention was on Himself. He knew that if Moses's eyes were focused on anything but the Lord, the mission ahead would overwhelm him and therefore produce excuses out of fear and discomfort. Then, after establishing the framework Moses needed, God told Moses to go to Pharaoh and bring the Israelites out of Egypt.

This was Moses's middle moment. This was a moment where Moses could live compelled by fear of the unknown. This was a moment where Moses could live compelled by a deep desire to avoid the discomfort that would come with following these instructions. Or this was a moment where Moses could live compelled by the character of God, the words of God, and the presence of God.

Moses knew God was calling him and now had to personally decide how he would respond. We would think that after hearing directly from God and being given insight into His heart and holiness Moses would be ready to go, no questions asked. Surely after clearly hearing the Lord call him by name and hearing about His record of faithfulness, Moses would be on board. This, though, was not the case. Instead, Moses said, "Who am I that I should go to Pharaoh and bring the children of Israel out of Egypt?" (Exodus 3:11).

Immense change had taken place in the last forty years of Moses's life compared to his first forty years. He had gone from being a royal in Egypt, receiving top-of-the-line service, to tending a flock and raising a family far away from anything he had previously known. Not thinking of himself as high and mighty, Moses had been sincerely humbled. He likely was aware of his unworthiness to partner with God in such great a task.

On the other hand, Moses's response to God probably didn't stem only from humility but also from shame and fear. God was telling Moses to go back to the very place from which he had fled for his life, to go back to the very place where he had murdered a man. Moses was being called to go back to the place that reminded him of what his life used to be. The chances are high that Egypt was a place that stirred up intense anxiety in his heart. Perhaps memories from Egypt that he had worked so diligently to erase were brought right back to the forefront of his mind in this conversation with God. It is likely that this conversation made Moses feel uncomfortable.

"Who am I?" was both a short and complex response, with many emotions and stories behind it.

This question is an amazing reply when coming from a place of reverence for God and humility before Him. When we humble ourselves in His presence, completely aware of our lowliness compared to His majesty, "Who am I?" is appropriate. The problem arises when we stop bowing in humility and start degrading ourselves in insecurity. This is when excuses emerge, because it is from this place that we begin depending on ourselves to do the work God has set before us. It is from this place that we walk by excuses instead of walking by faith. Humility stirs us up to walk by faith, while self-reliance can incline us to play it safe, avoiding any risks in our walk with God. Humility compels us to depend on God, while self-reliance tempts us to give excuses for why we are not able to go where God is saying "go."

God didn't respond to Moses's question by telling him how qualified he was for the job. He didn't hype Moses up in his own résumé. God didn't point to Moses as a means of giving him encouragement. On the contrary, God drew the focus back onto Himself by saying, "But I will be with you" (Exodus 3:12). God's comforting words for Moses were not about how competent he was, but how God's presence was enough. He was showing Moses that because He was with him, Moses had absolutely everything that he needed. God's response was so simple that we could easily neglect to acknowledge and even meditate on the power of it. And to be frank, we often do. We often overlook the weight of how wild it is that God is with us. If we really pondered such a miracle and believed His response to be true, our excuses would weaken at the knees, their screams silenced. If we had faith that God was with us in our everyday moments, how many more opportunities would we make the most of? How many more opportunities to love people would we be aware of? We would boldly live out our faith in the face of risk, knowing that God's presence is the safest place we could be. We would take action for the glory of God, knowing that He providentially meets us in the very spaces where our excuses typically have a field day.

To God's answer, Moses did not express a sigh of relief. He didn't say, "Well, in that case, count me in! How quickly can I get to Egypt?" Instead, he went on to his next concern, a concern that you and I often sit with. He thought, *What if the Israelites ask who sent me to lead them out of Egypt? What do I tell them?* As God's representative, it made sense to think through this potential situation. He wanted to know who exactly he was representing. What-ifs can help us be vigilant if responded to well. Though this "what if" question Moses framed was an understandable one, it was not anchored in faith. The fact that he would end up giving multiple excuses for backing out of this assignment after hearing God's reply shows us that Moses didn't ask this question with the full intention of speaking to the Israelites at all.

If we are not on guard, a "what if" mentality can keep us cautious to the point of living a cowardly life instead of a life compelled by Christ's love. At that point, these thoughts are no longer helping but hurting us, becoming another way to justify our desire to do what we would be more comfortable with. Like Moses, we can be concerned that people will ask us questions about our faith in Jesus, and through fear that we won't know what to say we hesitate to say anything at all. Because we don't know how someone will respond if we share the gospel with them, we think we might as well not initiate a conversation with them in the first place. The potential of being asked a question we don't know how to answer could either compel us to trust God in the moment, or send us down a spiral of more "what if" questions that only leave us paralyzed.

Moses had simply been told to go, that God would be with him, and that He would see it through. In the same way, God is also calling us to follow Him, trusting that He can give us what we need when we need it. We never have to worry about being equipped for His plan when we are following His lead. Even though no quantity of excuses could get in the way of God seeing His own plan fulfilled, excuses can get in the way of us partnering with Him in the plan. This is not to say that we shouldn't proactively ready ourselves for wherever God leads. It is to say, however, that we must not wait until we feel like we are in control before we follow Him.

We never have to worry about being
equipped for His plan when we are following
His lead.

Hudson Taylor is a good example of this. He served as a missionary in China in the 1800s and had a vision of reaching more people in China with the gospel. However, he was not able to move forward right away because anxiety pressed on him so heavily. He was in deep distress over both those dying in China without knowing Christ and the unassertive protection of those being sent to spread the gospel in dangerous Chinese territory. His mind probably rarely relaxed with his discordant concerns. Instead of focusing on the next step God was calling him to take to reach the people of China, Hudson was consumed with stress about how and if all the steps were going to work out.

Because of this worrisome struggle, he withdrew for some much-needed rest and insight. During that time, while he was walking along the beach, the Holy Spirit gave him understanding that led him to express, "The Lord conquered my unbelief, and I surrendered myself to God for this service. I told him that all responsibility as to the issues and consequences must rest with him; that as his servant it was mine to obey and to follow him."[3] Through trust and surrender, Hudson was given eyes to see his place as a servant to follow rather than as God to know all things. As servants of Christ, our responsibility is the same as Hudson's, whose responsibility was the same as Moses's: "to obey and follow" Christ no matter what.

The Lord's answer to Moses's question was not only a powerful message for the people of Israel to hear. It was also a greatly needed word of assurance to Moses. Moses didn't need to know if he had what it took; he needed to know that God did. God said:

I AM WHO I AM.... Say this to the people of Israel: "I AM has sent me to you. . . . The LORD, the God of your fathers, the God of Abraham, the God of Isaac, and the God of Jacob, has sent me to you." This is my name forever, and thus I am to be remembered throughout all generations. (Exodus 3:14–15)

The Lord told Moses to tell the people that the God who is self-existing, self-sufficient, and unchanging had sent him. The Lord even went on to affirm him, saying, "They will listen to your voice" (Exodus 3:18). And still, though God said the people would listen to Moses, Moses was not listening to God. The Lord's words were going in one ear and out the other as Moses retorted, "They will not believe me or listen to my voice, for they will say, 'The Lord did not appear to you'" (Exodus 4:1). Moses not only had excuses flowing off his lips, but his excuses were louder to him than the voice of God was. Moses was likely afraid of being unqualified and so caught up in what others would think that his excuses kept him from hearing and trusting the words God was clearly speaking. Still, even in the excuses, God patiently continued to show Moses that He was enough and that by His authority, this plan would prevail.

PURPOSE IN UNIMPRESSIVE MOMENTS

After listening to Moses's convinced insecurity, God asked him what was in his hand. This might have felt to Moses like God was changing the subject, avoiding the claim he had just made about how no one would listen to him. Not only that, but he was also probably unsure as to where God was taking the conversation, given the fact that the only thing in Moses's hand was a shepherd's staff.

God told Moses to throw his staff on the ground. When he did, his simple staff immediately became a snake right before his eyes. When Moses picked it back up, it returned to the form of a shepherd's staff. God said that would be a miracle He would perform in front of Pharaoh when Moses went to speak with him. This shepherd's staff was a way in which God intended to reveal His glory to Pharaoh. To Moses, the staff probably just seemed like a piece of wood, nothing more.

Similarly, so many years later, we can quickly believe our day-to-day lives are categorized as "unusable" by God because what we do might not seem established or important enough. We all have our own shepherd's staffs, if you will. We all have daily rhythms and roles. Whether we are stay-at-home moms or college students or night shift nurses, God has plans to reveal His glory to us and through us in those very places. Our current positions are not unusable in the presence of a miracle-working God. He wants us to make the most of where He has placed us. He is calling us to steward the titles and seasons and resources He has given us to bring great honor to His name. He wants to do miracles in our mundane world through our choice to faithfully make the most of the opportunities He gives us.

Surely after Moses saw a snake on the ground that was merely his staff just seconds before, he would be out of excuses and would just trust God and go. But no. His next excuse was one he would express more than once, meaning it might have been something he mulled over regularly. We all have that thought that rushes to the forefront of our minds when we think about stepping out of our comfort zone to be obedient to God. We all have that excuse, that reason why we shouldn't do what God is calling us to do. We all have that insecurity or that doubt that manifests itself into an ongoing excuse for why we most definitely cannot choose God in our middle moments. Moses's go-to excuse was his inability to speak well. He said, "Oh, my Lord, I am not eloquent, either in the past or since you have spoken to your servant, but I am slow of speech and of tongue" (Exodus 4:10).

What Moses probably wasn't considering was how perfect he was to carry out this mission. God had chosen the Hebrew man who was raised by Egyptians to speak to the Egyptians and lead the Hebrews into freedom. This seems rather fitting and shows that God had been working in and through Moses's life all along to prepare him for this moment and the moments to come. Moses knew the Egyptian language and was familiar with the culture. His heart burned with compassion, and he longed to see justice for his people. When we are focused on how to get out of what God is leading us to do, we overlook all the ways He has already equipped us for the task ahead.

Even still, the Lord didn't show Moses how prepared he was for this moment by stating the many ways Moses was fit for the call. God's response didn't consist of telling him how powerful a speaker he was or reassuring him that he had a way with words. He responded by telling Moses how good God is at being God.

Again, God pointed the attention to Himself. He said, "Who has made man's mouth? Who makes him mute, or deaf, or seeing, or blind? Is it not I, the Lord? Now therefore go, and I will be with your mouth and teach you what you shall speak" (Exodus 4:11–12).

Moses wasn't seeming to understand that God's sufficiency covered his speech. Because Moses thought he had to be enough, he wasn't finding relief in the promise that God alone was enough. God was not calling Moses to have a greater dependency upon himself to do this task. God was calling Moses to have a greater dependency upon God. When we live off excuses, it's as though we think God is expecting us to have certain qualifications to do what He is calling us to do, when actually He is inviting us to rely on Him and how qualified He is.

And after all of this, Moses finally said, "Please send someone else" (Exodus 4:13). The excuses had run out. The energy to carry on a conversation about possible outcomes and justifications for why he couldn't go to Pharaoh had dissolved. Moses finally exhaled the words that had probably been weighing on his soul for the entirety of their discussion. Getting to the bottom of it all, Moses just didn't want to go. He did not feel qualified and couldn't seem to trust that God was all that he needed.

GOD IS ENOUGH

Though Moses's story happened thousands of years ago, we have all had conversations like this with God to some degree. Our fear and doubt pile so high within our souls because our gaze is set on ourselves rather than on God. When all we can see are the reasons why we can't or don't want to go with God, out of our mouth come all the possibilities of failure, all the reasons why God has picked the wrong person, all the excuses. Moses's final plea exposed the reality that the problem was not the questions he could be asked. The problem was not that he didn't think the people would listen to him. The problem was not even that he didn't think he would do a good job. If we really get down to the bare roots of Moses's excuses, we see that he didn't trust God to be enough.

It's not that his excuses were outlandish. Many of his claims were understandable and legitimate. Being called to speak when you don't believe you're a good speaker is scary! To not know how all the details will come together can cause worry. To feel completely unqualified is relatable. To be intimidated by such a great call is understandable. Moses wasn't crazy for having these feelings and thinking through these things. His reasonings for backing out of God's call were fair, but that didn't make them worth leaning on. No matter how fair our reasons seem for backing out, God tells us to not rely on those reasons. Rather, He says to rely on Him in all our ways, and He promises to make our path straight (Proverbs 3:5–6).

Though it's unlikely for us to meet with God at a burning bush, we are all personally called by Him. As He did with Moses, God calls each of us by name with endearment to follow Him, and He does this each and every day. Just as Moses stood at the crossroads of a decision to either live compelled by excuses or by the heart of God, every single day we all stand in the face of opportunity to go with God or not. Excuses will be available all day long, so we cannot wait for them to go away before choosing to go with God. Otherwise, we may never go.

Just as Moses stood at the crossroads of a decision to either live compelled by excuses or by the heart of God, every single day we all stand in the face of opportunity to go with God or not.

Just as the Lord continually pointed back to Himself in response to Moses's excuses, He does the same with you and me. When our minds are clouded with thinking that we aren't educated enough, old enough, young enough, influential enough, or good enough to do what God has called us to do, He points us to how capable He is as God. He is I AM, and this means that He lacks nothing. He is not limited by any excuse we present before Him.

The apostle Paul wrote in the New Testament that "we have this treasure in jars of clay, to show that the surpassing power belongs to God and not to us" (2 Corinthians 4:7). When we begin to see our lives as jars of clay, held and shaped and filled by God, we will no longer be focused on reasons for God not to use us. Instead, we will be consumed with humble gratitude for all the ways He partners with us and equips us even while we are unworthy of Him.

If we were to step back and see that God knows every reason not to work in and through us, yet He still chooses to, our excuses would turn into reasons for praise. May the things that tempt us to give excuses be humbling reminders that we are mere jars of clay, unworthy of knowing God or making Him known at all, yet we get to and are called to. May our past excuses to not go all in with God now stir up excitement about how He might make His all-surpassing power known through us in the present and the future. We all have reasons to give excuses, but we also have a daily decision as to whether we will let those excuses compel us.

Warren Wiersbe said, "God can take an insignificant bush, ignite it, and turn it into a miracle."[4] The bush that Moses approached was merely a bush in the wilderness until God was in the bush. When God revealed Himself through the bush, then it was miraculous, something that we are still talking about thousands of years later. Before God was on the ground Moses stood on, it was just plain dirt, but when God was present, it became holy ground. What was just plain dirt turned into a space that required Moses to take off his sandals. Moses was a simple shepherd with a complicated past, but when he was with God and God worked in and through him, miracles happened, and the entire nation of Israel was set free from the bondage of the Egyptians.

In the same way, though we feel afraid, insignificant, and very much aware of the many reasons God could not and should not use us, He still desires to. He wants to take every part of us, even the parts of us that we think are only fit for excuses, and He wants to ignite us with His Spirit. He wants to do miracles in and through our lives that are far greater than what we could have ever imagined on our own. In our middle moments, we need to look to Him, surrender the excuses, and go. Miracles happen, the impossible happens, and all-surpassing power is revealed when God is present, because God is enough.

4

The Comfortable Christian

There are far, far better things ahead than any we leave behind.

—C. S. Lewis

I have definitely enjoyed the invention of the snooze button. Sometimes it feels like the morning comes too soon, the other side of my pillow is nice and cool, and the idea of a few more minutes to rest my eyes sounds so lovely. Staying in bed is relaxing, but choosing to get up is harder than I'd like to admit. Though there are wonderful things to be done when my alarm goes off, like spending time alone with God and getting a good workout in before my little girl wakes up, it is easy to want the comfort of my bed over the discipline of putting my feet on the floor and starting my day.

We all have had those mornings where we choose comfort over discipline. One of the worst feelings is finally deciding to get up only to notice that I hit the snooze button one too many times and I have just a handful of minutes to maybe grab a granola bar, find my keys, and beeline out the door. At that point, not only am I feeling groggy, but I also feel stressed because I didn't have time to prepare for the day and I am running late. Even though I know this and have experienced it too many times to count, I keep finding myself reaching to have a few more minutes in bed. It feels great, but after those short moments of drifting back to sleep, it goes from comfort to chaos. Choosing the comfort of bed regularly costs me the peace of my morning.

Research reveals the negative effects hitting the snooze button can have. According to sleep research, when we sleep through the night, we go through multiple sleep cycles including rapid eye movement (REM) and the three cycles within nonrapid eye movement (NREM),[1] lasting about ninety minutes.

Typically, if we are going to bed and waking up at a decent hour, our REM cycle is often wrapping up when our routine alarm sounds off in the morning. This means that when we choose to hit snooze, we are allowing our body to restart the sleep cycle, only to interrupt it a few minutes later. And if we push back the inevitable multiple times, truly falling asleep after turning off each alarm, then we are likely to experience sleep inertia, the condition that leaves us feeling quite groggy as we start our day.[2] On the flip side, studies have also shown that when we go to sleep and wake up at the same time each day, we are better equipped to have a healthy circadian rhythm.[3]

Unfortunately, knowing the negative effects of the snooze button doesn't take away the reality that staying in bed is comfortable. We can read all this information, yet the other side of our pillow is still satisfying to lie on. Having this insight doesn't make it easy to wake up when we hear our first alarm.

Knowing things alone rarely gives us the motivation to make change. We can know a lot of true and helpful information about our sleep and the long-term benefits of getting up at the first alarm, but that information cannot make the decision for us to get out of bed. We each get to choose comfort or discipline every single morning. We can choose short-term comfort or long-term well-being every day.

CHOOSING CONVENIENCE

Many of us, in a far deeper way, equate following God to waking up at the first sound of our alarm. We are hitting snooze in our relationship with Jesus by only loving others when it is convenient for us. We show up to church on a Sunday morning, but we live our day-to-day as though our everyday life is a completely separate thing from our faith in Christ. We make decisions that align with what makes us feel good and fits into our own plans instead of aligning our decisions with what would please God. There is no denial of ourselves in this way of living. This isn't actually following Jesus. We are choosing immediate comfort over the discipline of truly living compelled by the love of Christ. When our faith is compartmentalized from the rest of our life, we aren't living out our faith, we are simply adding church to our schedule. This is what it means to be a comfortable Christian—when we say we love God, but our daily life tells a different story.

Mark 10 tells the story of a man known as the "rich young ruler" who found out that Jesus was close by but on His way out of town:

> As Jesus was starting out on his way to Jerusalem, a man came running up to him, knelt down, and asked, "Good Teacher, what must I do to inherit eternal life?"
>
> "Why do you call me good?" Jesus asked. "Only God is truly good. But to answer your question, you know the commandments: 'You must not murder. You must not commit adultery. You must not steal. You must not testify falsely. You must not cheat anyone. Honor your father and mother.'"
>
> "Teacher," the man replied, "I've obeyed all these commandments since I was young."
>
> Looking at the man, Jesus felt genuine love for him. "There is still one thing you haven't done," he told him. "Go and sell all your possessions and give the money to the poor, and you will have treasure in heaven. Then come, follow me." (Mark 10:17–21, NLT)

Hearing what Jesus said, the man who was once eager, running to Jesus and kneeling before Him, now came face-to-face with a choice that needed to be made. Before him was an opportunity to stick with what he was familiar with and held so dear, or yield to the call of Christ, the call that required sacrificing his current comforts. This was a middle moment. Scripture doesn't tell us how long he pondered Jesus's invitation or how long he took to decide, but it does let us know that the man eventually turned away, deeply saddened because he realized that he wanted the instant gratification of his comfort more than he wanted Christ. He had found security in the things he possessed. He was known for being wealthy—it was his reputation. He was a man of authority, probably receiving much with great ease. And he was young! As far as he knew, he had so much life ahead of him. He probably imagined his life to be one of great status that he didn't want to risk losing.

Though this man knew a lot about God regarding the commandments to follow, the depth of his heart was exposed when challenged to leave his comfort. The purpose of God's commands was never to merely be checked off. God's commands were intended to reveal what is really in our hearts. When given the opportunity to get out of bed, put his feet on the floor, and literally walk with Jesus personally daily, the rich young ruler chose to hit the snooze button because what felt good in the moment mattered more.

A WARNING TO THE RICH

After the man decided to walk away, we read that Jesus turned and said to His disciples, "Dear children, it is very hard to enter the Kingdom of God. In fact, it is easier for a camel to go through the eye of a needle than for a rich person to enter the Kingdom of God!" (Mark 10:24-25, NLT).

Many of us might have checked out of this story already, thinking that we don't have anything to learn because we wouldn't put ourselves in the category of someone who is rich with many possessions. Rather than simply hearing the term "rich" and counting ourselves out, we must lean in to understand the heart behind what Jesus is saying. Jesus was addressing the fact that it is harder for the rich to lay down everything and follow Him because the more someone has, the more comfortable they become. The more comfortable they are, the more attached they get to the things that have given them such a life of convenience.

We love having more things, and we live in a world that encourages us to accumulate more things—more money, more status, more possessions, more of what seems to make life easier. However, when we love the things that we have more than we love God, it's easier for us to walk away from Him like the rich young ruler did. Though many of us wouldn't directly put it this way, we are more apt to think we don't need God when we are comfortable. And for some of us, there is a tension in our souls— a tension of love for God met with the belief that the things we have are able to meet our needs better than God can. Because of this tension, we often hold tightly to our riches instead of choosing to fully surrender and follow Him. It is safe to say that money is not the only form of wealth that can get in the way of our relationship with Jesus. When we are rich with attention from others, rich with status, rich with success, or even rich with an easy life, acknowledging our need for God can be incredibly hard for us. It is not that wealth, status, ease, and success are bad things. They can be good gifts from our good Father that we are to enjoy and steward for His glory. The problem arises when our love for these things surpasses our love for and devotion to the One who gave us those gifts in the first place.

King David wrote in Psalm 40, "As for me, I am poor and needy, but the Lord takes thought for me" (Psalm 40:17). How was he—a king—poor and needy? He had everything with the snap of a finger. He was served hand and foot. Why would he describe himself in this way if he was extremely wealthy?

David was not describing his material status; he was giving insight into the posture of his soul. David was poor and needy at heart, aware that apart from God he had nothing good (Psalm 16:2). He knew that he needed God. He knew that if the Lord was not with him, the greatest comfort would not be with him either.

It will be very hard for us to follow God in complete surrender if we think that apart from Christ, we are rich. To give up our comfortable faith and truly walk as His disciples means becoming poor in spirit, recognizing that nothing matters more than Him. Only then will we inherit the kingdom of heaven (Matthew 5:3).

It will be very hard for us to follow God in complete surrender if we think that apart from Christ, we are rich.

We have an inevitable tendency to go the easy route, thinking through what the most comfortable way to get by is and then choosing that. This is not because we don't want the best, it's just because we don't want the challenge. In school we often do what we can to merely pass the class rather than lean in to learn and excel in it. Many of us avoid going the extra mile in our work because simply getting the work done is enough for us. When conflict arises in our relationships, instead of embracing the difficulty of working through it, we stay in our comfort zones and miss an opportunity to grow closer with that person. Do we want to learn and excel? Do we desire to thrive in our work? Do we long for healthy depth in our relationships? Why, of course we do! We just don't want the challenges that come with seeing these results.

This desire to stay comfortable and avoid difficulty does not just show up in our classes and workplaces and relationships, it shows up in our faith as well. We have become okay with living out a mediocre faith. Though we would never want this to be true, many of us have become content with being average. Like the rich young ruler, our comfort matters more to us than being fully surrendered to Christ.

ALL IN

Although our salvation is secure through a one-time decision to sincerely put our faith in Christ, embracing the challenge of laying ourselves aside to boldly live out our faith is a decision set before us moment by moment, every day. Many of us aren't even aware that we are choosing comfort over Christ in our middle moments because we have become so acquainted with doing so that it doesn't even require a second thought. Picking the easy route is our second nature, and we don't even realize that we are following God conditionally—only when it fits our agenda and current desires. Though choosing immediate comfort now feels great, it also guarantees discontentment in the moments to follow, never fully satisfying the depths of our souls—never giving us the true rest only God can give.

Jesus's invitation for the rich young ruler to follow Him required that he sell all of his possessions and give the money to the poor. This call of followership required letting things go. For some of the disciples, following Jesus meant dropping their nets and leaving their boat. For Matthew it meant standing up and stepping away from the tax booth. For us, it might not look like selling everything we have or quitting our job, but it does mean that we open our hands, willing to let go of anything that gets in the way of our closeness with Him.

Jesus did not give the rich young ruler an option for the in-between, because there is no in-between. There is not an option of indifference when it comes to following Jesus, because following Him means embracing the challenge of sacrifice, denying ourselves, and picking up our cross. Period. Jesus didn't say that the rich young ruler could follow Him and keep living the life he was living. In the same way, He doesn't tell us that we can follow Him while also keeping a tight grip on our five-year plan. He doesn't tell us to follow Him and stay in the relationship that doesn't glorify Him. He doesn't invite us to follow Him and say it's okay that we only obey the scriptures that make us feel good. There is no middle ground in our middle moments. We either choose Christ or we don't. We are either with Him or we are not. So many of us are missing the joy of knowing Christ because we aren't going all in. In seeking to avoid anything that might be unsettling, we are avoiding the greatness of what it means to be a Christian. Boldly living out our faith calls us to walk out of our comfort zone and through hard things. We cannot live compelled by our love for comfort and the love of Christ at the same time. Confidently living out our faith is much more than wearing the label of Christianity as a shield, and it is more than growing up in a Christian home. Being His disciple is more than praying a prayer. For many of us, we have prayed for Jesus to be the Lord of our life, but nothing in our life has changed because we aren't living as though He is our Lord. We are living as though comfort is.

Being a Christian carries a weighty reality. So weighty that Jesus tells us to pick up our cross daily (Luke 9:23). For one to pick up their cross, they are committing to die—die to living for themselves—and be brought back to life by the power of the Holy Spirit so that they may live for Christ who died for them and was raised. This is extremely uncomfortable and is no small ask. It is uncomfortable to put the desires of our flesh to death. It is uncomfortable to love others as Christ first loved us. It is uncomfortable to confess our sin. It is uncomfortable to repent. It is not easy to change, but if we aren't changed by the gospel, have we really given our lives to it?

The gospel compels change. The death, burial, and resurrection of Jesus is worth more than only obeying Him when it is convenient for us. He is worth more than talking about Him only with those we know will agree. He is worth nothing less than our whole lives. He is worth everything. Even when it's hard and requires that we don't do what would feel so good in the moment, He is worth following. He is worth trusting. Even when it's uncomfortable and our friends could respond with great offense, let's love them enough to share the message that can save their souls. Even when it means letting go of control, let's respond to God's call in complete surrender. Even when it is challenging, let's be obedient to God and bring our sin into the light. The more we submit to Him, the more comfortable we will get with choosing the uncomfortable route. Moment by moment, as we choose Christ, we will discover how much better His way is—we will discover the rest He has to offer our souls (Jeremiah 6:16). We will discover that walking with Him, though not always comfortable, is always comforting because in our willingness to embrace discomfort, He embraces us.

JESUS UNDERSTANDS

Christ not only calls us to do the hard things and is with us in the hard things, but He also has embraced a greater sacrifice of comfort than any of us ever have or will. God doesn't call us to do what He didn't exemplify. Jesus is calling us to lay down our lives to live for Him, and did He not do that for us? Jesus was with the Father in heaven as they enjoyed the presence of each other, in the most comfortable position one could imagine. They were together in glory. Yet, to do the will of the Father (John 6:38) and "for the joy set before Him" (Hebrews 12:2), He:

> did not consider equality with God as something to be used to his own advantage; rather, he made himself nothing by taking the very nature of a servant, being made in human

likeness. And being found in appearance as a man, he humbled himself by becoming obedient to death—even death on a cross! (Philippians 2:6–8, NIV)

Jesus sacrificed his comfort for the eternal glory of His Father, for the eternal hope we now have in Him. Christ saw the delayed reward worth laying down the instant gratification for. And as His followers, we are to entirely give ourselves as He did. When we give our life to Christ, our life ought to daily look more like Him and less like living for temporary comfort. As Paul said, we are to be "imitators of God" (Ephesians 5:1, CSB).

> When we give our life to Christ, our life
> ought to daily look more like Him and less
> like living for temporary comfort.

INSTANT GRATIFICATION VS. DELAYED REWARD

When I am in the middle of a workout, muscles shaking and lungs burning, it is incredibly tempting to cut my reps short and not go as hard. In that moment, when everything hurts and I so badly want to take the less challenging route, I have the choice of momentary ease or delayed gratification. The decision to persevere makes me stronger, and the joyful satisfaction of drinking my protein shake, enjoying deep stretches, and releasing endorphins afterward is incomparable. These delayed reliefs and long-term results require the giving up of instant gratifications, but it never fails to be worth the sacrifice.

What the enemy doesn't want us to know and what the desires of our flesh don't tell us is that when we choose to forgo instant gratification, we are promised something even greater, something that lasts. After the rich young ruler turned away feeling sorrowful, Jesus turned to the disciples and said, "There is no one who [surrenders everything] for my sake and for the gospel, who will not receive a hundredfold now in this time [what they gave away] and in the age to come eternal life" (Mark 10:29–30). Jesus guaranteed that going all in with Him leads to everlasting life and blessing and satisfaction. He promised that the instant gratification we lay down now for the sake of the gospel doesn't come close to the reward we receive in return. Notice that the pillars of comfort the rich young ruler was unwilling to lose are now nonexistent, as he is no longer rich, he is no longer young, and he is no longer ruling. He walked away from Jesus sorrowful because he had many possessions, but now those possessions add up to nothing of real worth. What he made his everything equates to nothing in light of being a disciple of Jesus Christ Himself, who is the light, the life, the way, the truth, and the One in whom we find the only comfort that really lasts.

When we lose our life for Christ, we actually find it. We find a greater comfort than anything this world could offer. We find a greater satisfaction and contentment than anything the riches of this life could provide. Isn't that just like God? To only have what is best for His kids? If only we really trust Him—trust not only that He is worthy of our whole selves but also that He is doing a good, loving work amid the challenges and discomforts.

The present treasure of knowing Christ and the future gratification of eternity is what we savor as we embrace the sacrificial life of following Him now. When we are standing in our middle moments, flooded with desire for temporary comfort, we can choose Christ:

> For this light and momentary affliction is preparing us for an eternal weight of glory beyond all comparison, as we look not to the things that are seen but to the things that are unseen. For the things that are seen are transient, but the things that are unseen are eternal. (2 Corinthians 4:17–18)

So, we must ask ourselves, which comfort matters more? Does the comfort of going our way matter more, or does the comfort of walking intimately with Jesus matter more? Our answer to this question doesn't only impact us today, but it impacts us when these days on earth are all said and done.

Even now, you may be ready to put your feet on the floor, to no longer live for temporary comfort, yet almost immediately you are being met with condemnation for the countless times that you have turned away from Christ like the rich young ruler did. Maybe right now your conviction and excitement is being greeted with regret for how you have chosen to roll over and stay comfortable day after day. This shame that you are feeling is not from God. This weight of fear that is enveloping your mind is not of His Spirit. Scripture says that God's *kindness* leads us to change our ways (Romans 2:4). It says that sorrow from God leads us to repentance, *not* to paralyzing guilt (2 Corinthians 7:10). What a beautiful day this is, filled with new opportunities to go with God. He is not rejecting you for what your yesterday looked like. Rather, He is calling you to Him, delighted to see that you are responding to His invitation with a yes.

BE READY

Just as hitting the snooze button one too many times can lead us to experience a chaotic morning, having zero time to feel ready for the day, if we keep hitting snooze on the call to boldly live out our faith, we are not going to be ready when Jesus comes back. When He returns, our souls will be in chaos as we realize that we missed what mattered most. We are going to look up and discover that our attention was consumed by worthless things that gave us instant gratification that didn't last rather than eternal satisfaction that we were made for. It will be clear to us that the things we held so closely hold no weight in comparison to the glory of God. Yes, it is by grace through faith that we are saved, but in the end many of us will come to find that our reward is barely anything because we wanted the cold side of our pillow more than we wanted the value of putting our feet on the floor. We will get a wakeup call only to find that we wanted our own comfort more than we wanted to please God with our lives— more than we wanted to see lost souls be found, more than we wanted to use our gifts to serve the Church—more than we wanted to walk in a manner worthy of the calling we had been given.

Scripture says that Jesus is going to come at an hour and a time that we don't know, therefore we must be watchful and ready always. Considering His return ought to compel us to reject the temptation of staying comfortable in our faith. Because if we are honest, is a comfortable faith even faith at all? Are we walking by faith if we stick with a lifestyle that is merely convenient for us? According to Christ, that is not what it means to wholeheartedly walk with Him. A life compelled by comfort is not a life focused on eternity, it is a life focused on the temporary.

Just as there are wonderful things to be done when we hear our alarm go off in the morning, there are wonderful things to be done in the kingdom of heaven. We don't have time to delay. We don't have time to roll over. Paul told the church in Ephesus, "Be very careful, then, how you live—not as unwise but as wise, making the most of every opportunity, because the days are evil" (Ephesians 5:15–16, NIV). It's time to wake up, put our feet on the floor, and boldly live out our faith. As Christians, it is time for us to embrace the challenge of sacrificing our desire for instant gratification and start living compelled by the things of eternity.

5

A Personal Relationship

For what higher, more exalted, and more compelling goal can there be than to know God?

—J. I. PACKER

Before my husband, Josh, and I started dating, we were in the same friend group in college. Not long into our freshman year, a group chat was created called "Table for 20," because one time, twenty of us college kids showed up at a restaurant to eat together before going to a hockey game, and the name simply fit perfectly. As a group, many of us would go to church together, grab meals together, study together—there were very few things Josh and I didn't do together as friends with that amazing crew.

Our college campus was located amid the Blue Ridge Mountains. The daily view was one that could easily stop anyone in their tracks, absolutely captivated by the beauty of the peaks and valleys. On one particular fall evening, I got a text from Josh saying, "Hey, when the leaves start changing colors, we should go on a hike. Then we can do something with the group." I stood in my dorm room frozen. Elation set the rhythm of my heartbeat and then nerves quickly took the excitement's place. Back and forth they took turns. This text message was not sent in the group chat. This was a note delivered to me. Josh specifically wanted to go on a hike with me and only me. I had spent plenty of time with Josh before. We had shared so many hours eating in the dining hall, hanging out at football games, and studying in the library with friends. But this was different. This was different because this was personal.

When things get personal, they hold a greater weight, they have a different type of impact on our lives. On the night I was moments from being saved by Jesus, I got down from my bed and walked over to my bookshelf. Among the many books was one devotional I had never even opened before. It was called *Devotions for the God Girl*. In the introduction it said, "When other people are sleeping, the God Girl is waking up to wait and watch for [God, because she] wants more than anything else to hear from him."[1] These words gripped my heart in such a way that I had to do something about it. I had to respond. I wanted to know God in that way more than I wanted anything else. I wanted to know Him in a way that was personal.

Just as Josh wanted to personally spend time with just me rather than getting together with the whole friend group, so was I with God in this moment. This moment for me was not just because Christianity was the faith of my parents. This was not just because Jesus was the right answer in Sunday school class. This was personal between just me and God. I yearned to personally seek His face. I longed to hear His voice for myself. The mere thought of such intimacy with God stirred my affections deeply. So I closed the devotional and tears streamed down my cheeks as I poured my heart out before the Lord. I told Him how badly I wanted to know Him. I remember saying, "God, I want to know You. I want to know what makes You happy and I want to know what makes You sad." As I spoke with Him in a posture of both surrender and readiness, it felt like celebratory fireworks were going off in the core of my soul. I was overwhelmed, knowing that I was beginning a personal, lifelong adventure of knowing God.

EVERYTHING CHANGES WHEN IT'S PERSONAL

The reason Jesus will turn many away when the end comes is not because they didn't have a certain church attendance or show up to enough community service projects. Jesus will turn many away because they never personally knew Him. It will be because they did not have a relationship with Him. He will claim that He does not know them. In one sense this is refreshing to hear that God desires closeness and friendship with us. In another sense, to say the least, this is an urgent call for us to see that Christianity is not a box to check off, but a one-on-one relationship to be experienced in fullness with God Himself. We cannot enduringly live compelled by something we haven't personally experienced. To live compelled by the love of Christ, we must personally know the love of Christ. To unashamedly live out our faith in Jesus, we need to intimately know Jesus. Otherwise, our excitement to live for Him can only last so long and only go so deep before deflating.

In John 4, Jesus met with a woman at a well who, according to the information we have in Scripture, had a rough history. Because she was drawing water from the well in the middle of the day by herself, rather than with other women in a cooler hour, we can assume there was something going on causing her to isolate, causing her to probably be socially ashamed. Jesus could have met with anyone on that day, and He chose to meet with her. He not only chose to meet with her, a woman. But He chose to meet with her, a Samaritan woman, which was doubly frowned upon in this culture. In so many moments throughout Scripture, Jesus showed that His desire for a personal relationship with people is not limited by their gender, ethnicity, past mistakes, or cultural norms.

After talking with the woman for a while, Jesus revealed to her that He knew her past and even went on to show her that He was the Messiah. Amazed, the woman left her water jar at the well, ran back into town and said to the people, "Come, see a man who told me all that I ever did. Can this be the Christ?" (John 4:29).

The woman's immediate response to a personal encounter with Jesus was to set down the weight she was carrying and go tell others about Him, inviting them to meet Him too. Getting water that would leave her thirsty again didn't matter anymore, as she dropped her jar and went straight back into town. There was no sense of shame or sorrow in her words as she told anyone who would listen to come and see the One who knew the ins and outs of her past.

Notice that she didn't pause and contemplate how much experience she had in speaking in front of people. She didn't question whether she knew enough Scripture. Nor did she stop to consider how much influence she had before running back into town to proclaim a message about Jesus. No, she had personally met with Jesus; therefore, she was compelled to tell others about Him.

Far too often we get caught up in reasons why we think we can't share our faith or live out our faith boldly. Unlike the Samaritan woman, we think about how many followers we have, how long we have been a Christian, or how much of the Bible we have read before we talk about Jesus at all. Because these are the things we ponder, we often feel unqualified, and we shy away from opportunities far more than we make the most of them.

Many people believed in Jesus through the woman's testimony. Imagine how many people the Lord desires to bring to Himself through your boldness to run into your own town, your campus, your home, your workplace—and share your testimony of personally knowing Jesus.

KNOWING GOD VS. MERELY KNOWING ABOUT HIM

Not only did many people believe in Jesus, but they also told the woman, "It is no longer because of what you said that we believe, for we have heard for ourselves, and we know that this is indeed the Savior of the world" (John 4:42). When the people personally listened to Jesus and saw Him for themselves, they were convinced that Jesus was God.

There is a great difference between hearing about God secondhand versus coming to see God for yourself. Commentator William Barclay wrote:

> We might know every verdict ever passed on Jesus; we might know every Christology that human minds have ever thought out; we might be able to give a competent summary of the teaching about Jesus of every great thinker and theologian— and still not be Christians. Christianity never consists in *knowing about* Jesus; it always consists in *knowing Jesus*. Jesus Christ demands a personal verdict.[2]

Being in a close relationship with God is much more than just knowing a lot of information about Him, though knowing about Him is essential. How else can we grow in a personal relationship with God unless we know about Him? The problem that sometimes arises with knowing a great deal about God is that it doesn't always fuel a deeper relationship with Him; rather it just makes us more scholarly.

The religious leaders of Jesus's day knew more about the Scriptures than anyone else. They had studied it frontward and backward pretty much their entire lives, but when they looked at God square in the eye, they didn't even know it was Him. More information does not always produce greater intimacy. Jesus knows that when we personally believe Him to be who He says He is, we will live compelled by His love no matter the cost. It has to get personal. Life change happens when things get personal. To boldly live out our faith in Him unconditionally, we each must come to Him ourselves, listen to Him with our own ears, see Him with our own eyes, and personally know Him in our own heart.

Life change happens when things get personal.

When talking about knowing God, be encouraged to know that a relationship with Him is not one-sided. Many of us have had relationships with people where we pour out so much, but no love is reciprocated. And oftentimes our faulty earthly relationships can be the lens through which we see our relationship with God. But God is different. It is not as though we have to work our fingers to the bone as we invest in a relationship with God and never get a response. God does not ghost us. No, in fact God made the first move and has never stopped pursuing us. Nor will He ever stop. He knows us completely. He sees us fully and yet He stills draws near to us asking questions, enjoying time with us, and delighting in hearing our hearts. He is a compassionate, kind God.

Over and over again in Scripture, God makes it abundantly clear that He wants us to know Him. Jesus prayed to the Father, "This is eternal life, that they know you, the only true God, and Jesus Christ whom you have sent" (John 17:3). God spoke through the prophet Jeremiah saying, "Let him who boasts boast in this, that he understands and knows me" (Jeremiah 9:23–24).

Some of Peter's last words to the church were, "Grow in the grace and knowledge of our Lord and Savior Jesus Christ" (2 Peter 3:18). God said to Hosea, "My people are being destroyed because they don't know me" (Hosea 4:6, NLT). As though it is the cry of God's heart, in the book of Ezekiel alone He spoke a total of fifty-eight times, that all His actions were for the purpose of His people knowing that He is the Lord. God does not stand far off, giving no opportunity to know Him. In fact, He loves us so much and demonstrated His great love with utmost perfection by coming to us personally.

This reality alone ought to bring us to an altering halt. The Lord of lords, the King of kings, the Creator of heaven and earth loves you and me with such a passion that He would sacrifice to the greatest degree so that we might truly know Him. "What is mankind that you are mindful of them, human beings that you care for them?" (Psalm 8:4, NIV) is the humble response this lavishing love demands because we, sinners, do not deserve this kind of pursuit.

We turned our backs on God, we have gone against His Word, we have betrayed Him, and yet He responds by making a way for us to be restored to the purpose for which He made us—knowing, enjoying, and glorifying Him. There is no greater love than this (John 15:13). God does not love simply out of choice but out of His very nature. He is love (1 John 4:8). Out of the very nature of who He is, He chose to come from heaven and dwell among us. Wanting us to know Him, He made a way for us to see "his glory, the glory of the one and only Son, who came from the Father, full of grace and truth" (John 1:14, NIV).

Not only did He make Himself known to us by putting on flesh and living with us for a time, but He did so without fault. He lived perfectly to be led to a cross, "to be sin for us, so that in him we might become the righteousness of God" (2 Corinthians 5:21, NIV). So that in Him, we might know God. Jesus said, "I am the way and the truth and the life. No one comes to the Father except through me. If you really know me, you will know my Father as well" (John 14:6–7, NIV).

We can believe all of this to be true and still find ourselves wondering, *What does it even mean to really know God?* Yes, it is through Christ that we can know Him, but what does knowing Him look like?

FEAR GOD, KNOW GOD, LOVE GOD

Really knowing God cannot take place apart from fearing Him, and truly loving God cannot happen apart from knowing Him. The three go together; in fact, they are inseparable.

Solomon wrote, "The fear of the LORD is the beginning of knowledge" (Proverbs 1:7, NIV). There is frequently much confusion that arises with the concept of fearing the Lord. We tend to wrestle with how personally knowing God and being afraid of Him could possibly go together. They seem to be at odds with one another. In his book *Rejoice and Tremble,* Michael Reeves encourages us "to rejoice in this strange paradox that the gospel both frees us from fear and gives us fear."[3] By the power of the gospel, we no longer have to live in fear's thrall, afraid of the wickedness in the world or of death. At the same time, the gospel reveals that grace has been bestowed upon us by a God who had every right to release His wrath on us forever. While this does lead us to take on a posture of fear, it is a different kind of fear from that which our minds initially go to.

As children of God, we do not have to live in a fear associated with dread and terror. Rather, we get to and are called to live in what is called "filial fear." Filial fear is childlike, coming from a place of knowing God as both Creator and as a personal, loving Father whom we delight in pleasing. So to have a filial fear of God is to have an awe of Him that is rooted not only in humility, but in belonging and safety and love as well. Charles Spurgeon expressed it like this:

> Gazing upon the vast expanse of waters, looking up to the innumerable stars, examining the wing of an insect, and seeing there the matchless skill of God displayed in the minute; or standing in a thunderstorm, watching as best you can, the flashes of lightning, and listening to the thunder of Jehovah's voice, have you not often shrunk into yourself, and said, "Great God, how terrible art thou!"—not afraid, but full of delight, like a child who rejoices to see his father's wealth, his father's wisdom, his father's power—happy, and at home, but feeling oh, so little![4]

To fear God as His sons and daughters is to recognize who we are in relation to who He is and therefore give Him the worship He is due. When we fear God, we have a better perspective of Him, and therefore, our intimate knowledge of Him grows.

Those who fear the Lord are joyful, they are blessed, and they are friends of God (Psalm 112:1, NLT; Proverbs 28:14; Psalm 25:14, NLT). Notice that the fear of God and enjoyment in Him go together, hand in hand, all throughout the Scriptures. We are able to rejoice in our relationship with God and grow in friendship with Him the more we see Him rightly and revere Him as is His worth.

So often we claim that we know God, but these words are not followed up with a life that reflects fear of Him or love for Him at all. The Israelites also struggled with this, and the Lord said of them, "This people draw near to me with their mouth and honor me with their lips, while their hearts are far from me, and their fear of me is a commandment taught by men" (Isaiah 29:13).

These people did not fear God in their own hearts; therefore, they did not truly know Him. They might have known what fearing God meant by definition, but they did not know what it meant by experience. Just as we often know the right words to say that give us the appearance of godliness, it is possible that we don't actually have a personal closeness with the God we are so eloquently speaking of.

David wrote of God, "For you will not delight in sacrifice, or I would give it; you will not be pleased with a burnt offering. The sacrifices of God are a broken spirit; a broken and contrite heart, O God, you will not despise" (Psalm 51:16–17). The Lord is not looking for us to show and tell all that we know about Him and all that we have done in His name, for this is not the same as personally knowing Him. What He's looking for is a heart that trembles before Him. He is looking for the lowly one who is very much aware of their need for a Savior. He is looking for hearts that fear Him. If we have hearts that fear the Lord, then our words of love for Him will much more likely be backed up with action because they will be coming from a place of personal conviction, true intimacy.

TO KNOW HIM IS TO LOVE HIM

Again, the Lord said to His people, "Your love is like a morning cloud, like the dew that goes early away. . . . For I desire steadfast love and not sacrifice, the knowledge of God rather than burnt offerings" (Hosea 6:4, 6). God is not saying that He doesn't care about what we do. Rather, He knows better than anyone that what we do overflows from what is in our hearts. He knows that if we truly know Him and love Him then we will be compelled to be obedient to Him, living a life that pleases Him.

The author of Hebrews later wrote, through Christ:

let us continually offer up a sacrifice of praise to God, that is, the fruit of lips that acknowledge his name. Do not neglect to do good and to share what you have, for such sacrifices are pleasing to God. (Hebrews 13:15–16)

Be assured that Scripture is not contradicting itself here. God is showing us the order in which a life compelled by His love takes place. A life compelled by the love of Christ is carried out by hearts that are genuinely close to God. From that place their lips sincerely praise Him, and their hands and feet serve in His name. The more we tremble in His presence, the more we know Him, and the more we know Him, the more we grow in love with Him.

Not only does a lack of fear of God keep us from growing in love and intimacy with Him, but our naïveté in thinking that enjoying God is reserved for when we get to heaven also keeps us from delighting in Him right here, right now. Knowing God is not something we have to wait to experience one day in eternity.

David wrote of God, "He has saved me from death, my eyes from tears, my feet from stumbling. And so I walk in the LORD's presence as I live here on earth!" (Psalm 116:8–9, NLT). As we live here on earth we can know God, meaning that we can learn who He is, experience His presence, and enjoy closeness with Him as we would our greatest friend! This is one of the most astonishing realities of the gospel. He has gifted us with the joy of walking in His presence and knowing Him more and more even right now as we go about our everyday lives. We get to personally know Him today.

Proverbs 3:6 gives us insight into how we can practically get to know Him today: "In all your ways acknowledge [God], and he will make straight your paths." The word "acknowledge" in this verse means to know or to recognize. How would our lives look different if we were to notice God in all our ways? What would change about the moments that fill our day-to-day if we were to actively know God as we experienced them?

GETTING TO KNOW GOD

If someone were to approach me and ask how they could further get to know someone they liked, I would encourage them to spend time with that person—grab a bite to eat, go on a walk, ask them questions about their life, get to know their friends, etc. Oftentimes, as in our romantic relationships, we overcomplicate our relationship with Jesus. Practically, we wonder how to get to know Him further, how to learn more about Him and grow in our relationship with Him. To this curiosity, I would give similar advice. We need to spend time with Him, we need to talk with Him, and we need to get to know people who are close with Him.

For us to know Jesus more personally, we need to spend time with Him. I will never forget one particular day, Josh and I both had so much going on. We saw each other all throughout the day, were together with large groups of people, and had little conversations here and there. But at the end of the day Josh said, "I missed you today!"

I said, "Aw, I missed you too!"

Though we had been with each other during the day, we had not gotten to have quality time together, just the two of us. I kept thinking about the simple conversation we had about missing one another. A few days had passed, and I told Josh that his small comment so simply described how I had been feeling with the Lord lately. From trying to get a workout in the early morning, to caring for my sweet baby throughout the day, to working during her nap times, to even just having a mind preoccupied by a million things, it felt like I was missing quality, undivided time with God.

Reflecting on what Josh said, I told the Lord, "I miss You," and I felt as though God said, "I miss you too." It wasn't in a condemning way, but in the way my husband spoke to me.

Just as Josh and I spent so much of the day together but still missed each other, God is with us all day long welcoming and waiting for our direct attention. Scripture says that there is nowhere we will go that His Spirit will not be (Psalm 139:7). Still, we can miss Him. Not in harshness, but in love, God invites us to not merely spend time with Him in passing. Instead, He invites us to enjoy Him, share quality time with Him, and sincerely be mindful of Him. He invites us to abide in Him.

TALKING WITH GOD

A woman in the Bible named Rebekah was pregnant with twins. Scripture says that the babies "struggled with each other in her womb" (Genesis 25:22, NLT). After she felt them struggling, "she went to ask the LORD about it." Though this is amazingly simple, there is a life-changing lesson embedded in her response to the situation she faced. Her choosing to go to the Lord about this matter may not seem like much, but how often do we go to the Lord about the many things that consume our day? The English Standard Version translates this verse as "she went to inquire of the LORD." This word "inquire" means to intentionally and expectantly seek out. Rebekah prayed in faith. This was a mundane middle moment that held great meaning.

More often than not, our middle moments of choosing to trust God or not show up in the seemingly quiet situations that have the chance of directing our thoughts into a downward spiral. Rebekah could have gone down the easiest route—the route of worry that comes with thousands of "what if" scenarios, fearful of her babies' health. She could have let herself become anxiety ridden because of the weight the uncertainty brought her as a new mom. Instead, her response to the wrestling of her babies is such a beautiful example of how we can know God in all our ways throughout our everyday moments. To some this might have been too silly and small a thing to pray about, but nothing is too little or too mundane to go to God with. God loves when we seek Him with care. He delights in us coming to Him expectantly. Just as our own personal relationships grow stronger the more we spend time with one another, so is it that our personal relationship with God becomes closer the more we talk with and listen to Him.

SPENDING TIME WITH GOD'S FRIENDS

We need to get to know those who are also walking with Him. Typically, if we are getting to know someone we like, who that person's friends are says a lot about them. We can learn more about a person by spending time with their close people. In the same way, we can learn a lot about Christ by spending time with people who are friends with Christ.

David wrote that we are blessed when we choose to "not walk in step with the wicked or stand in the way that sinners take or sit in the company of mockers" (Psalm 1:1, NIV). Being thoughtful and intentional about who is in our inner circles is wise because our closest people are guaranteed to influence our daily, personal relationship with God. The people we choose to regularly do life with will majorly impact our walk with God.

In Psalm 101:6, David said, "I will search for faithful people to be my companions" (NLT). The context of this verse is that David was looking throughout the land for people to serve him. Though we are not looking for people to serve us, we can apply this to our lives by also looking for faithful people to walk with us as we walk with God. We can apply this by being actively involved in our local church, studying God's Word in community, and growing in relationship with other believers. Through being surrounded by people who are living compelled by the love of Christ, we are taught, championed, and held accountable to do likewise. The number of times people in my life have been used by God to draw me closer to Himself are too many to count.

Solomon wrote, "Two are better than one, because they have a good return for their labor: If either of them falls down, one can help the other up. But pity anyone who falls and has no one to help them up" (Ecclesiastes 4:9–10, NIV). We were not meant to walk with God in isolation, but in community. When we have faithful people walking beside us, we can be encouraged and sharpened as we grow in our relationship with Him (Hebrews 10:24–25; Proverbs 27:17).

It is common for us to think that getting to know Jesus is limited to having our Bible opened at a particular time in the morning with a cup of coffee in hand. Nothing more and nothing less.

What if I told you that time with Him is fully in that space, but it is also when we are talking with Him as we do the dishes? It is also when we are meditating on His Word while waiting to pick up our kids in the school carpool line. It is also when we stop to encourage our neighbor while we are out on a walk with our dog. It is also when we are with friends, reflecting on how our week has gone. It is also when we are using the gifts He has given us to serve others. It is also on a Sunday morning as we pause to praise Him.

Just as we would grow in a personal earthly relationship through getting together one-on-one, sharing meals, sitting in homes, gathering with friends, and going out into town, so is it that we grow in our heavenly relationship with Jesus by intentionally talking with Him and being with Him everywhere we go all throughout our day. Day by day, in the quietness and in the busyness, we can grow in our personal relationship with Christ. As Paul prayed over the church of Ephesus, so do I pray over us today: "I keep asking that the God of our Lord Jesus Christ, the glorious Father, may give you the Spirit of wisdom and revelation, so that you may know him better" (Ephesians 1:17, NIV). Because the more we know Christ, the more we are compelled by His love in our middle moments.

Day by day, in the quietness and in the
busyness, we can grow in our personal
relationship with Christ.

6

It Is Written

As the outward man is not fit for work for any length of time unless he eats, so it is with the inner man. What is the food for the inner man? Not prayer, but the Word of God—not the simple reading of the Word of God, so that it only passes through our minds, just as water runs through a pipe. No, we must consider what we read, ponder over it, and apply it to our hearts.

—George Müller

As I was growing up, my dad would write notes and leave them in places for me to see and be encouraged. His little messages were sometimes silly and sometimes sentimental but always abundant with the truth about my identity and how much he loved me. Whether he would write a note and tape it to my bathroom mirror or send a sweet text my way, years later I still think on the words he shared. When I am having a hard day, doubting if I am valued or beautiful, I remember what he told me and am comforted. I know that even though his notes were written a long time ago, the messages on them are still just as true.

This intentional act my dad did while I grew up was a small picture of what our heavenly Father has done. Not only did God make the first move to have a relationship with us by sending Jesus, but He also has made Himself known to us through words penned on paper. Just as the words my dad wrote me are still true today, God's words written thousands of years ago have not lost their power or relevance; His words are both timely and timeless.

But are we taking the time to read and know the words He has personally spoken? Based on a study done by *Christianity Today*:

In 2021, about 50 percent of Americans said they read the Bible on their own at least three or four times per year. That percentage had stayed more or less steady since 2011. But in 2022, it dropped 11 points. Now only 39 percent say they read their Bible multiple times per year or more. It is the steepest, sharpest decline on record.[1]

Why is this the case? Why is it that we have so much access to God's Word, yet our time in it is decreasing? Could it be that we don't fully realize what Scripture is and the miraculous gift it is to have such easy access to it?

My husband and I recently went on a trip to Italy. The place where we stayed had a local farm, which made every meal quite splendid to say the least. On this local Italian farm there was a beehive, and each morning we were given the opportunity to take parts of a honeycomb to enjoy at breakfast. There are few things I have experienced that tasted better than that fresh, sweet, dripping honey. While sitting at breakfast with Josh, savoring that golden treat, I remembered what David wrote in Psalm 19:10 about the Word of God. He said that it is "sweeter also than honey and drippings of the honeycomb." More delightful than raw honey from a rustic valley in Tuscany are the living and active words of God Himself.

Scripture is literally God putting pen to paper through different authors in history. He personally has spoken words to fill an entire book with information about who He is, what He is like, and how the story of our lives fits into the grand story He has written for His glory. And to this, we are saying, "I'll give it a few days out of my year." In a world that is constantly changing, God's Word is reliable and rock steady. We can count on every word to be fulfilled, and we can depend on every promise to prove true. And to this, we are saying, "I just don't have time to fit it into my schedule."

It is by His Word that we learn how to live compelled by His love, where we learn what it even means to be a Christian. So if we are professing to be believers but we are neglecting to spend time in the Word, it is no wonder we aren't practicing what we proclaim. How can we put action to something we don't even know?

Contrast our ambivalence with the actions of people in other countries around the world who can get their hands on only the smallest amount of Scripture. They memorize what they have, considering it greater than a gold mine, and feel overwhelmed with gratitude just to read a portion of it. All the while, we have more means to access Scripture than ever before—from countless Bible apps, to Bibles found on coffee tables and nightstands in our homes, to the good ol' World Wide Web. It's almost as though we are so used to the Bible being easy to reach that we have lost the joy of reaching for it.

It's almost as though we are so used to the Bible being easy to reach that we have lost the joy of reaching for it.

Our familiarity with it has numbed us, and we have grown blind to the beauty right in front of us. Our problem is not misunderstanding how good the Bible is for us. Our problem is not access to the Scripture itself. Our problem is not insufficient time to spend in it. So why then is it not a priority in our lives? Why is our view of its importance on such a sharp decline? Three main reasons we are not valuing and delighting in God's Word are distractions in our lives, busyness in our routines, and shame in our souls. Let's dig into each of these.

DISTRACTIONS

Let's be honest, it is easy to let our attention be pulled from one thing to another in just a matter of moments. Especially with social media. The constant ability to view content and be enter-tained sets up the perfect opportunity for distraction all day long.

As a *Harvard Business Review* study on the effect of endlessly scrolling on social media found:

> These platforms are designed to trap viewers in a social media rabbit hole: They offer bite-sized content that makes it easy to quickly consume several videos or posts in a row, then often automatically start playing similar videos, reduc-ing the potential for interruptions.[2]

There's a continual intent of entertainment in social media, and this has produced in us an expectation of constant, immedi-ate pleasure. Whereas the intent of Scripture is to know God and be equipped to live compelled by His love. Its purpose is not to entertain us. So when we get bored or don't quite understand what we are reading as quickly as we would like to, finding other things to fill our time often seems more appealing. What if we were to slow down in the face of the temptation to get distracted from God's Word? I love these lines in a poem by Clarence Ed-ward Flynn:

> Discoveries are missed each day
> By men who turn too soon away.[3]

Distraction is robbing us of discoveries. Turned off by bore-dom and turned away by distraction, we neglect to linger in the

Word of God that would eventually lead to the beholding of treasures with a far greater depth than any entertainment could ever offer. Research has shown that "the 'typical' social media user now spends 2 hours and 23 minutes per day using social platforms."[4] If this is the case, social media is getting two and a half hours of our day and God's Word is getting a few days out of our year. It's safe to say that distraction is keeping us from delighting and discovering.

When we notice ourselves getting distracted from spending time in God's Word, we are nearing a middle moment—a moment where we get to decide if we will give in to the distraction or lean into the discipline, expecting a discovery—a discovery of greater closeness with the one who breathed the very words we are reading. Distractions will always be present. There will always be a reason for not spending time with God in His Word. The feeling of delight to read the Bible will not always be bubbling over, and discoveries will not always come in the timing we desire. But the distractions and the uncomfortable feelings do not take away from the necessity of getting in the Word and letting the Word get in us. David wrote that we are blessed when we choose to put our "delight in the law of the LORD, meditating on it day and night" (Psalm 1:2, NLT). Delighting is a disciplined decision we get to make daily, and, with the help of the Holy Spirit, we can even do it when feelings come and go.

BUSYNESS

As a mom and a wife who is leading a ministry daily, I do not believe busyness to be a bad thing. These days are full. Not only that, but each season brings changes and new rhythms. My day-to-day rhythm does not look like it did when I was single in high school. Nor does it look like it did when I lived in a house with my best friends in college. My schedule certainly changed when I was in my early postpartum months, waking up every three hours with my newborn. As each season comes, adaptation and grace comes with it. There will be days when we have an abundance of time to spend in God's Word, and there will be other days when we are making the most of the fifteen minutes we do have. One is not more spiritual than the other. It is the intentionality to prioritize being in the Word that matters. Our seasons and rhythms may shift throughout our lives, but may the discipline and delight we have for God's Word remain. Steadily abiding in His Word keeps us steady when life feels as though it's constantly changing.

Jesus set a beautiful example for us of how to prioritize time with God amid busyness and a full schedule. Scripture mentions a time when "the report about [Jesus] went abroad, and great crowds gathered to hear him and to be healed of their infirmities" (Luke 5:15). In other words, Jesus was busy. This is just one verse of many that tells us about crowds of people coming to Jesus, wanting to hear from Him, be near Him, and be healed by Him. Day in and day out, He was with people, serving and loving and teaching. His busyness was picking up by the day as word about Him spread. More people were pulling for His attention than ever before. His schedule was full of appointments. He had many places to be, plenty of people to see, and many meetings to attend.

It would have been easy for Jesus to claim He didn't have time to step away, but Scripture tells us that "he would withdraw to desolate places and pray" (Luke 5:16). No amount of busyness could keep Him from prioritizing time alone with the Father. His response to the busyness of life was to carve out purposeful time with God. Jesus was dependent upon the Father and showed us that nothing is more important than intimacy with Him. Oftentimes we think we don't have time to sit and be in God's Word, but what we don't realize is that being with Him in His Word directly impacts how we navigate whatever busyness our day might hold. Spending moments with God in His Word refocuses us on what matters most and renews our minds, so we are ready for whatever the next moment brings.

If spending quality time in God's Word isn't intentionally marked down in our daily schedule, we are not as likely to do it. Sometimes we don't see spending time in God's Word as important enough to mark on our daily calendar because it doesn't feel as productive to us as does cleaning the house, finishing the assignment, or responding to the emails.

We often associate productivity with something we can check off a to-do list, and while we can check off having read the Bible on a particular day, the heart transformation is not transactional like that. Spending time in God's Word doesn't promise a productivity we can always immediately see or feel. We don't often read the Bible and notice an instant change in our character.

It is normal not to understand God's Word right off the bat. Experiencing a tangible closeness with God the moment we begin reading is not a guarantee every time. Because this is the reality, reading the Bible doesn't fall in line with our desire of trying to get as much done as we can in as little time as possible. Reading His Word, understanding it, and growing by it is a lifelong journey that summons us to show up daily as the Spirit leads us and works in us in the ways only He can. It takes investment and patience and endurance, as things worthwhile typically do.

On the flip side, just as we don't always immediately see the positive impact God's Word has on our lives, we don't always immediately see the negative impact that neglecting God's Word has on our lives either. In our productivity-driven mindsets, we tend to take note of the consequences that come from neglecting daily responsibilities.

The priorities we have on our tasks seem to be based on what feels most pressing in the moment. Reading the Bible doesn't have frequent deadlines as our school assignments and work projects do. Even at home, for example, if we don't take out the trash, our trash cans will start to overflow, and the house will begin to smell. Yet, if we don't open up the Bible, it just continues to sit pretty on the bookshelf, with no immediate consequences that our eyes can see. Just as the fruit of being in God's Word is borne over time, so too are the outcomes of forsaking it. The effects of putting off reading God's Word may not show up instantly, but this daily decision makes itself known greatly over time. Neglecting God's Word will eventually have an impact like the trash that was never taken out, filling the house of our hearts with a foul odor that seeps into every area of our lives.

SHAME

Shame keeps us from delighting in God's Word by leading us to believe that the God we are reading about doesn't love us. We are convinced that we have disappointed Him and that there's no way He will see us again with gracious eyes. Every time we open the Bible, the only thing on our minds is what we regret the most. Even more so, we are certain that the thing we are embarrassed about is the first thing on God's mind when He thinks about us. No wonder we don't delight in time with Him. In this case, it makes sense that we are choosing to occupy our time with anything but being alone with the God we believe despises us. No wonder fear of condemnation is the only thing on our minds when we do manage to get in His Word.

We have a very real enemy who is described as the accuser and father of lies (John 8:44). The last thing he wants is for us to be in the Word because he knows that Scripture is the truth. And when we know the truth, we are set free—set free from his lies, set free from the shame of our past, and set free to live compelled by the love of Christ! Satan doesn't want us to grow closer to the God who promises that there is "now no condemnation for those who are in Christ Jesus" (Romans 8:1). Of course he doesn't want us looking to the Lord because he knows that if we do, we shall be radiant, never covered with shame (Psalm 34:5). It is through

God's Word that we can discover Jesus's actual heart toward us and, by the power of the Spirit, live out what we know to be true.

FILLED WITH THE TRUTH

Looking back, I am deeply grateful that my dad showed me that Jesus wanted a personal relationship with me and that he challenged me to read the Bible. I could have surrendered to the Lord that night but left my Bible on the bookshelf to continue collecting dust. I'm overjoyed that I didn't, because knowing God and submitting to His Word go hand in hand. By opening God's Word daily, I not only grew in knowledge of Him, but my heart also became full of the truth. And this is important because what we are full of spills out when we are hit by difficult moments. It is when we find ourselves between a rock and a hard place that we discover what our hearts are really full of, what we are actually living compelled by.

While sitting in the bleachers and encountering the bullies, it wasn't just having a Bible verse memorized that steadied me. His words had been settling in my soul like a firm foundation, preparing me for whatever storms were to come my way. Whether we are aware or not, what we fill ourselves with today is always an act of preparation for whatever tomorrow brings.

Whether we are aware or not, what we fill ourselves with today is always an act of preparation for whatever tomorrow brings.

Filling ourselves with God's Word does not mean that we simply know it. What's the point of knowing it but not doing anything with it? To be filled with Scripture means to know it and live it, to be changed from the inside out because of it.

That November night at the basketball game, receiving adamant comments from guys and girls saying they didn't like the way I looked, I was equipped to recall God's Word that declared I was fearfully and wonderfully made in His image (Psalm 139:14; Genesis 1:27). I knew that God told me I didn't have to be afraid of what people thought because He was with me. I knew God had spoken that His joy was my strength (Nehemiah 8:10).

But knowing all these things isn't what compelled me to respond with love in that middle moment. Yes, knowing what God said was essential, but if I didn't believe and put action to what He said, this story would have had a very different ending. I had to choose to lean on God, trusting that He really was with me, being my ever-present help in times of trouble (Psalm 46:1, NIV). I had to commit to believing what God said about my worth and beauty and let that be the voice that determined my confidence. Knowing the truth is amazing, but if we don't put it to practice, we aren't experiencing the authority it holds and the freedom that it gives.

LOVE AND OBEDIENCE GO HAND IN HAND

Jesus told us that if we love Him then we will obey Him. The two cannot be separated. If we aren't living out the Word of Christ, we cannot live compelled by the love of Christ. They go together because it is His Word that guides us in the way of Christ, guards us against the things seeking to steer us from boldly living out our faith, and grounds us when the storms of life blow in.

In Matthew 7:24–27, Jesus said:

Everyone then who hears these words of mine and does them will be like a wise man who built his house on the rock. And the rain fell, and the floods came, and the winds blew and beat on that house, but it did not fall, because it had been founded on the rock. And everyone who hears these words of mine and does not do them will be like a foolish man who built his house on the sand. And the rain fell, and the floods came, and the winds blew and beat against that house, and it fell, and great was the fall of it.

The man whose house crumbled when life got challenging heard God's Word but never took it seriously. He knew what Jesus said but he never put the rubber to the road, living differently because of it.

James wrote that we must:

Be doers of the word, and not hearers only, deceiving [ourselves]. For if anyone is a hearer of the word and not a doer, he is like a man who looks intently at his natural face in a mirror. For he looks at himself and goes away and at once forgets what he was like. (James 1:22–24)

When we hear God's Word but don't yield to His guidance, we aren't actually building our lives on Him, though many of us think we are—hence why James let us know we are deceiving ourselves. And if we are living like the man who built his house on the sand, it makes sense that we are crumbling, choosing what makes us more comfortable when the going gets tough. If we are not aligning our lives with God's Word then it is no surprise we are collapsing under peer pressure, quieting down about our faith in Jesus, and believing what everyone says about us.

God does not call us to know and obey His Word for the purpose of simply adding more rules to our lives. Scripture says that those who love God obey Him, and that His commands are not burdensome (1 John 5:3). The commandments of the Lord give us life (Deuteronomy 30:16). They bring freedom and blessings (James 1:25). By them, we are "thoroughly equipped for every good work" (2 Timothy 3:17). In choosing to meditate on His Word day and night, we are promised to be like a tree planted by streams of water. Our fruit will yield in season, our leaves will never wither, and whatever we do will prosper (Psalm 1:2–3). God wants the best for us. He wants the house of our lives to remain standing when storms come. In calling us to obey His Word, He is calling us to Himself, He is calling us to the best. He is calling us to find the life we were made for, a life filled with and led by His love. In instructing us to follow the good and ancient path, He is calling us to discover rest for our souls (Jeremiah 6:16).

JESUS IN MIDDLE MOMENTS

Jesus does not just call us to hear and live out His Word, but He also gets what it's like to stand in moments of pressure to do the exact opposite. Scripture says that He is not "a high priest who is unable to sympathize with our weaknesses, but one who in every respect has been tempted as we are, yet without sin" (Hebrews 4:15). He shares in our humanity. Just as we do every day, Jesus had to decide if He would choose His own comfort or choose obedience to His Father. He had an opportunity either to lean on excuses or to trust that His Father was more than enough. As storms blew toward the house of Jesus's life, He had to decide what His perspective would be. He understands what it's like to face a challenge, needing to decide if God's Word will be lived out or not.

Right before Jesus began His three years of ministry, He traveled from Galilee to the Jordan River, where He found His cousin John (widely known as John the Baptist) baptizing many people. Jesus too wanted to be baptized by John, so He made His way to the water. After John baptized Him, something incredible happened. As Jesus was coming up out of the water, "the heavens were opened to him, and he saw the Spirit of God descending like a dove and coming to rest on him; and behold, a voice from heaven said, 'This is my beloved Son, with whom I am well pleased'" (Matthew 3:16–17). Jesus personally saw that God was with Him and specifically heard His Father affirm Him.

The Holy Spirit then led Jesus into the wilderness to be tempted by the devil. In other words, Jesus was led into the wilderness where middle moments were soon to expose what He had been building His life upon, what He had been filling Himself with. While in the wilderness for forty days, Jesus fasted and prepared for the ministry that was ahead of Him. While going forty days without eating anything, Jesus was very hungry and in a vulnerable state. It was in this place of hunger and vulnerability that the enemy eased in with his schemes. He said, "If you are the Son of God, command these stones to become loaves of bread" (Matthew 4:3).

Notice that the very first thing we read to come out of the enemy's mouth were words the Father had already spoken over Jesus. Only, these words uttered by Satan likely carried a different tone—a tone of craftiness, a tone with a deceitful agenda. The enemy would have probably loved for this one-liner to plant doubt in Jesus's mind about what the Father had clearly affirmed in Him. Jesus had been told by the Father that He was God's Son, and He had personally seen that God was with Him when the dove rested on Him. And here comes Satan, brewing up a storm to crash into Jesus's house. He challenges Jesus's identity. He calls Him to prove that He really is who God says He is. He invites Him to go out of God's way to satisfy His hunger.

This was not a strategy Satan used just this one time with Jesus in the wilderness. He uses this with us every day. He longs for us to second-guess our true identity. He craves for us to look anywhere but to God for our needs to be met. He used this with me in the bleachers, wanting me to question if all I had read and meditated on in God's Word leading up to that moment was even true. With a simple statement seasoned with doubt, he aims to create confusion so maybe, just maybe, we will stop living compelled by the love of Christ and start living compelled by a lack of trust in God and a greater dependence upon ourselves.

Jesus was standing at a crossroads. He could take the bait and begin to doubt who He was. He could give in to the comfort of using His power to get food instead of trusting God to provide Him with everything He needed. Or, He could recall the words His Father had just spoken to Him—that He was God's Son, that He was loved, that He had the approval of His Father, and that He was not alone. He could recall the Scriptures He had learned growing up (Luke 2:40, 52). He could choose to display His trust in God by being obedient to His Word. However He responded would reveal what He was filled with, because it is out of our heart that our mouth speaks (Luke 6:45). It is from the heart that we make decisions (Proverbs 4:23). Jesus replied, "It is written, 'Man shall not live by bread alone, but by every word that comes from the mouth of God'" (Matthew 4:4). God's words weren't just something for Jesus to memorize; they were His fuel, they were what He lived by. He clung to what He was filled with.

Because Jesus recalled the truth that His Father had spoken, you can too by the power of His Spirit. When the enemy is tirelessly working to lure you away from what is true about your identity, in the authority of God's Word you can declare with finality that you are a "[member] of the household of God" (Ephesians 2:19), "a temple of the Holy Spirit" (1 Corinthians 6:19–20), made "in the image of God," kept by God (Psalm 121:7), God's workmanship in Christ Jesus (Ephesians 2:10), planned and loved and chosen before the foundation of the world was laid

(Ephesians 1:4–5), called out of the darkness and into marvelous light to proclaim God's excellencies to the world (1 Peter 2:9). When the enemy is seeking to destroy your faith, inclining you to lean on your own understanding, with bold assurance you can announce that the Lord is your shepherd and you shall not want (Psalm 23:1), that He is faithful to "supply every need of yours according to his riches in glory in Christ Jesus" (Philippians 4:19), that His good Spirit is in fact leading you on level ground (Psalm 143:10), and that He indeed is where your help comes from (Psalm 121). And we could keep going. Friend, when you begin to know and believe the truth of who God is and who you are through His Son, you will be able to stand in the face of the enemies lies with certainty and stability. But the enemy wasn't finished. He tried to take Jesus out twice more in the wilderness, tempting Him to change His perspective and choose comfort over obedience to the Father, all while giving Him excuses for why doing so would be okay. Yet time and time again Jesus quoted Scripture saying, "It is written," in response to these middle moments. Jesus knew He was in a spiritual battle, so He fought with spiritual weapons, taking every temptation captive and making it obedient to the truth. And He was able to do this because He knew and believed what the truth was.

KNOWN BY HEART

Baking is one of my favorite hobbies. It is a way I mentally rest and unwind. Baking always brings people together because everyone loves dessert, and it is pure fun for me. My first choice when considering what to bake on any given day is definitely chocolate chip cookies. I remember when I first started baking what is now my go-to recipe. Before each and every step, I would read the full list of directions over again to ensure that I was doing everything correctly. I'd do one step, then go back to the cookbook. I'd do another step, then skim the page once more. But one day, I noticed that I wasn't having to go and see how much flour I needed, or how high to set the oven, or if the butter was supposed to be room temperature. I realized on that day that I didn't have to go to the book anymore because the book was in my memory. I knew how to make those cookies by heart.

And that's what Jesus had done with the Word of God. He had gone back to the book so many times that He not only knew it, but He also was confident in it! He knew it so well that He was able to call out the lies of the enemy with it and win His battles! He had studied the Word and meditated on it so much that He didn't have to pull out a scroll in the wilderness while standing in the storm with Satan. The Words on the scroll were imprinted on His heart and He could therefore recall them by memory. When the going got tough, the truth came out because the truth was what filled Him.

When we are in middle moments, what we have been building our lives on will be exposed. The things we have been filling ourselves with will be revealed. We will recall from memory all that we have been constantly looking at and thinking on.

The three times we read of Satan tempting Jesus were not the only times. In fact, Scripture says that Jesus "was led by the Spirit in the wilderness for forty days, being tempted by the devil . . .

And when the devil had ended every temptation, he departed from him until an opportune time" (Luke 4:2, 13). The entirety of Jesus's time in the wilderness involved temptation, and Satan kept looking for opportunities to lead Jesus astray after that. Jesus was constantly choosing to trust God. Over and over again, He made the decision to not only recall the Scriptures but also to submit to them. Likewise, though we have been set free from the power of sin through the blood of Christ, the fight against spiritual darkness is continual for us until Jesus returns. Middle moments are bound to happen in some way every day. No matter who we are, we all face times of difficulty. We all have an enemy who hates us. We all daily wrestle in the opposition between the Spirit and the flesh. In the hard times, like Jesus, we get to decide whether we will cling to the Scriptures and live out our faith, or not.

May distractions and busyness and shame no longer keep us from the closeness with God and the authority that is found in knowing and living out His Word. May the Word of Christ dwell in us richly (Colossians 3:16), transform us by the renewal of our minds (Romans 12:2), and be our response to whatever comes. Like Jesus, may we respond to trials and temptations with "It is written," confident that those words will never fail us!

We will not be taken out by the evil one, nor will we give way beneath the storms of life, if God's Word determines the life that we live. For it is through being equipped with God's Word that we will live compelled by the love of Christ.

7

Who Is My Neighbor?

I speak to everyone the same way, whether he is the
garbage man or the president of the university.
—ALBERT EINSTEIN

When I was in school, I typically would power walk through the
halls to try to get to class on time at the last minute. My teachers
knew why I was regularly running late. My high school was made
up of thousands of students. This meant that between each class,
crowds of people would pour through the double doors that con-
nected the stairwell to the hallway. Each day I would get to
the top of the stairs, take hold of the door handle, stand off to the
side, and tell people how beautiful and wonderful they were as
they passed through. Sure, it was normal for me to be a tad late to
my next class, but tardiness didn't matter as much to me as telling
those students they were loved, even if they only heard it once
each day while walking through the double doors.

Years later, well removed from that echoing stairwell and
those student-packed halls, people still come up to me in random

places and say, "Hey, I just want you to know that you held the door open for me and told me I was the bees' knees back in high school. It meant so much and I just want to say thank you."

These people aren't telling me that they remember how I played in a soccer game. They aren't coming back saying how impressed they were with my GPA. They aren't going out of their way to talk about a speech I gave in a student council meeting. No, they are coming back to tell me that they still remember when the door was held open for them, when a smile was personally directed at them, and when kind words were spoken to them.

In high school it can be so easy to think that grades and popularity and making the team and having a boyfriend or girlfriend are most important, leading us to miss the hearts of people we walk by and sit next to every day. This mindset doesn't go away when we graduate.

After high school, we quickly become consumed with our five-year plan, how fast we can climb the corporate ladder, what successes we have, who we are going to marry, and sometimes just how we can get through the day without being interrupted. Season after season, we can be entirely fixated on what's next or what's in it for us. All the while, though these things seem awfully significant in the moment, are they most important? Years later, at the end of our lives, will we look back and say that those were the things we needed to be dialed in on?

We will make sacrifices and process decisions in life based on what we are convinced is paramount. The kind of life we live illuminates what we believe is of greatest importance. I believe that those who came back to me years after high school, saying what they remembered was feeling loved, were bringing to light what actually matters most.

> The kind of life we live illuminates what we believe is of greatest importance.

THIS IS MOST IMPORTANT

Matthew 22:35–40 tells the story of an interaction between Jesus and the Pharisees:

> One of them, an expert in religious law, tried to trap him with this question: "Teacher, which is the most important commandment in the law of Moses?"
>
> Jesus replied, "'You must love the LORD your God with all your heart, all your soul, and all your mind.' This is the first and greatest commandment. A second is equally important: 'Love your neighbor as yourself.' The entire law and all the demands of the prophets are based on these two commandments." (NLT)

Jesus said that if we were to get right down to it, the most important thing in our life as a Christian is love. How is it possible that thousands of years' worth of prophecies and teachings can be summed up into two simple statements? Jesus said that every bit of the Old Testament can be summarized in this: Love God and love people.

We cannot live a life compelled by the love of Christ apart from loving people, because they go together. Jesus said, "If you love me, you will keep my commandments. . . . This is my commandment, that you love one another as I have loved you" (John 14:15; John 15:12). To love Jesus is to love others as He first loved us. Love is essential. It cannot be skipped over, worked around, or avoided. If we go our whole life without grasping the gravity of its value, we would in fact have missed what is most important. Jesus even said, "By this everyone will know that you are my disciples, if you love one another" (John 13:35, NIV). Our love for one another tells the world that we are with Jesus.

Our love for one another tells the world that we are with Jesus.

When Paul was writing his first letter to the church of Corinth, the Corinthians were missing what was most important. They were convinced that their spiritual gifts superseded everything else. Even more so, they specifically believed that if they had the gift of speaking in tongues, they were top-of-the-line—extra special and extra close with God. They basically thought that the type of spiritual gift they had indicated their personal level of spiritual maturity. They believed this because it "was universally accepted in the Hellenistic world that some were especially close to the gods. Usually this closeness was supposed to be manifested by trances, ecstatic speech, and other unusual or bizarre forms of behavior. All this was taken as a special spiritual endowment."[1]

Because of the cultural belief, the Corinthian church was majorly influenced to view their gifts through that lens. This led them to lose sight of what Scripture actually points to as the top priority. It is insightful to know this background because it is the context from which Paul was speaking when he continued writing the verses we often hear quoted at weddings or see painted on signs hanging in people's homes.

The next verses are some of Paul's most famous words:

> If I speak in the tongues of men and of angels, but have not love, I am a noisy gong or a clanging cymbal. And if I have prophetic powers, and understand all mysteries and all knowledge, and if I have all faith, so as to remove mountains, but have not love, I am nothing. If I give away all I have, and if I deliver up my body to be burned, but have not love, I gain nothing. (1 Corinthians 13:1–3)

Paul was helping the church see what really mattered. He was emphasizing to them and to us that love is the greatest measure of spiritual maturity. How sincerely a person loves speaks more to their closeness with God than anything else ever could.

We could become scholars of the Bible. We could sell everything we own and show up at the soup kitchen to feed the homeless every weekend. We could put our life on the line for our faith. We could have the gifts of speaking in tongues and proph-esying boldly. But according to God through Paul, we would just be making obnoxious noise, gaining nothing, if we are without love. What we do has no significance if our deeds are lacking love.

We could give away everything as Jesus called the rich young ruler to do. We could move forward to conquer the promised land in faith, as Caleb and Joshua did. We could speak the words of God to one another in high esteem, as Moses did with Pha-raoh. But without love, what have we really profited? If all our faith is applied and our gifts used so that we may boast in ourselves—rather than for the purpose of love—what is the point? This is why living compelled by the love of Christ is not a call to merely do more acts of charity or do more in faith. Paul wrote, "The only thing that counts is faith expressing itself through love" (Galatians 5:6, NIV).

LOVE IS

So if love is key, then it is necessary to have clarity on what love even is. Today's definition of love seems to get foggy. It has be-come more common for love to be basically boiled down to agreeing with one another. We have become a people that feels unloved if we are offended in any way.

Love can also be identified as a mere feeling we experience. Because of this, we tend to be loving only to those we like. Once the happy, romantic feelings fade, we opt out. This type of love is conditional.

The love Jesus said was most important is not the type of love that is based on a feeling, nor is it based on the need to be agreed with. The love that our faith is meant to express, the love that Jesus said summed up the Scriptures, is known as agape love. Agape love is deep, unwavering endearment. It is a decision we make despite how we may feel. Agape love is unconditional, sacrificial, and committed. This is the love that God has called us to. This is the love we are compelled to live by. This is the love that, at the end of our lives, will be what was of greatest importance.

The Corinthian church, at the time Paul addressed them, was not only emphasizing the gift of tongues unnecessarily, but they were also envious of one another. They were taking each other to court rather than working out their differences with grace, and they were living in a way that stirred up division among themselves. Because they didn't see love to be of utmost importance, their lives didn't reflect love. So Paul did more than explain to them how vital love is, he also went on to give them a definition of it. He wrote:

> Love is patient and kind; love does not envy or boast; it is not arrogant or rude. It does not insist on its own way; it is not irritable or resentful; it does not rejoice at wrong-doing, but rejoices with the truth. Love bears all things, believes all things, hopes all things, endures all things. Love never ends. (1 Corinthians 13:4–8)

In describing love, Paul described Christ.

Christ embodied every attribute associated with love because it's who He is. When we look at the life of Jesus, we are looking at

ove on perfect display. When we wonder what it means to love
well—when we are curious about what love even looks like—we
can look to Jesus.

The apostle John wrote, "In this is love, not that we have loved
God but that he loved us and sent his Son to be the propitiation
for our sins" (1 John 4:10). God's love for us was never determined by our deserving it. In fact, we are least deserving, and still
He chose to love us completely, holding nothing back. He lavished His love on us, pouring it into our hearts through His
Spirit (Romans 5:5). We will never go a day in our lives not being
loved by God. To experience this love He has so bountifully given
ought to shake us up. His love is not the kind to leave us the same
as it found us. His love changes us from the inside out, not ending with us, but continuing through us and compelling us to live
differently.

THE UNEXPECTED ANSWER

One day there was a lawyer who came to Jesus and, with the intent of testing Him, said, "Teacher, what shall I do to inherit eternal life?" Jesus replied by asking him what the Scriptures said,
and the man answered, "You shall love the Lord your God with
all your heart and with all your soul and with all your strength
and with all your mind, and your neighbor as yourself." Jesus affirmed that in living out that command, the lawyer would inherit
eternal life.

Unsatisfied, and trying to see if there was a way to justify how
he viewed and treated people, the lawyer asked, "And who is my

neighbor?" (Luke 10:25–29). He likely hoped that the answer would be his own Jewish people—those who, for the most part, thought like him, looked like him, and shared the same culture as him—no one else.

How often have we done this? How often do we try to justify how we feel about loving people and excuse the partiality we show? Without even realizing it, every time we engage with people, we decide whether they are our neighbor, and often the answer is determined by how we feel about them. Typically, we are particular about who our neighbors are. We tend to subconsciously think this way because, simply put, some people are harder to love than others. Some people feel like an inconvenience. Some have hurt us. Some aren't as easy to get along with. And some make us feel uncomfortable because they don't look like us, talk like us, or think like us. We would prefer our neighbors to be only those who are easy to love, only those we like.

In response to the lawyer, Jesus told a story about a man who was on his way from Jerusalem to Jericho. While traveling, that man was robbed, stripped, and beaten. Those who assaulted him had left him half dead where they had found him. Jesus said, "Now by chance a priest was going down that road, and when he saw him, he passed by on the other side. So, likewise a Levite, when he came to the place and saw him, passed by on the other side" (Luke 10:31–32).

These two men didn't pass by because they didn't notice the wounded man. They both saw him and still chose to continue their journey around him. According to the Jewish law, a person was considered ceremonially unclean if they even touched someone who was dead. The priest and Levite, in charge of duties in God's temple, considered their cleanliness more important than the care this man needed. In doing so, they missed the whole point of God's Law—they missed what was most important.

How many people are sent our way, but we miss the opportunity to love them because we think they are in our way? How many people do we overlook because they might not look important enough to us? How many people do we forgo acknowledging because we are convinced that our image and to-do list matter more?

But Jesus introduced a third traveler to the story. He said, "A Samaritan, as he journeyed, came to where he was, and when he saw him, he had compassion" (Luke 10:33). The Samaritan man—one who was least expected to stop for the injured man because Samaritans were despised by Jews—proceeded to take care of the man lying on the path and saw to it that he had everything he needed to get well.

All three of these men were in a middle moment as they walked past the man left half dead on the road. Either they could choose to give excuses as to why they couldn't show compassion, or they could live out their faith by loving well (because to live out your faith is to love well).

Jesus asked the lawyer, "'Which of these three, do you think, proved to be a neighbor to the man who fell among the robbers?' He said, 'The one who showed him mercy.' And Jesus said to him, 'You go, and do likewise'" (Luke 10:36–37).

The lawyer asked Jesus who his neighbor was, but Jesus didn't give an exact answer. Jesus was not dodging the man's question;

rather Jesus went deeper and addressed the bigger issue from which the question came. The lawyer wanted to know whom he did and did not have to love. Notice that Jesus didn't give the lawyer a list of qualifications regarding who his neighbor was or what his neighbor looked like. Jesus didn't tell him that his neighbor had a certain political stance, came from a specific economic status, or was of a particular ethnicity. He didn't even say that his neighbor had to be of the same religion—and this is Jesus speaking.

Rather, Jesus showed him what it meant to be a good neighbor. Instead of talking about who qualified as a neighbor, he directed the question back to the lawyer and told him the kind of neighbor he must be. Jesus pretty much answered the lawyer's question of who his neighbor was by saying, "Yes." No matter the person, what they look like, where they have come from, Jesus said that they are our neighbor, and we are to show them compassion. Why? Because Jesus first loved us and showed us the greatest compassion of all.

The Lord doesn't look at people as we often do. Our knee-jerk reaction is to look at the outward appearance of someone, and from that alone assume a great deal about them and determine how we will treat them. But God looks at the heart (1 Samuel 16:7). Imagine how different our everyday lives would be if we looked beyond the surface level and considered the hearts of people. What amazing things the Lord would do in us and through us if we were consumed by a desire to find all the ways we could love people well instead of being distracted by all the reasons why certain people don't deserve our love. This is agape love—love that has no conditions, no qualifications, and no agenda. The point of this story is not so that we can nail down who deserves our love and who doesn't. It is to show us what it looks like to love like Christ—what it looks like to be compelled by His love.

This is agape love—love that has no conditions, no qualifications, and no agenda.

I had fair reasons to not consider those who bullied me to be my neighbors. I would have been justified had I hated them or held grudges against them. But because of Christ, I was compelled to love them. One might say, "Come on, Emma, Christ couldn't have made that big of a difference in your life to be the reason you responded with grace to those who were mean to you." But it is true. Christ changes everything, including how we see and value people. Even the ones who give us every reason to overlook and despise them. If we were to only love those who love us, then we would not be living compelled by the love of Christ. Instead, we would be living compelled by the actions of others. Again, Christ is our example and He loved us when we hated Him and rejected Him. We gave Him every reason to condemn us, but He decided to show us compassion. Now there is no other appropriate response but to love others in return.

The apostle John wrote:

We love because he first loved us. If anyone says, "I love God," and hates his brother, he is a liar; for he who does not love his own brother whom he has seen cannot love God whom he has not seen. And this commandment we have from him: whoever loves God must also love his brother. (1 John 4:19–21)

Being in a personal relationship with God results in a life marked by love for people; there is simply no separating the two. Has knowing the love God has for us changed the way we treat others?

Being in a personal relationship with God
results in a life marked by love for people;
there is simply no separating the two.

Even though faith expressing itself through love is most important, and even though loving people and being a follower of Jesus go hand in hand, we can't adequately love people on our own. No matter how hard we try, we cannot be loving neighbors by our own strength. On our own, we are selfish and impatient. On our terms, we are passive and unforgiving. Even if we were to give all the love we have, we could not love others as Christ loved us—not apart from Him.

God will never call us to do something that doesn't involve our entire dependency on Him. Jesus told His disciples, "I am the vine; you are the branches. Whoever abides in me and I in him, he it is that bears much fruit, for apart from me you can do nothing" (John 15:5). It is only through Christ that we can live compelled by the love of Christ.

We might wonder how we abide in Christ and what that even means. Well, John dove into it more later in his life, saying, "By this we know that we abide in him and he in us, because he has given us his Spirit" (1 John 4:13). Through faith in Jesus, we have the Holy Spirit who lives in us, helping us, guiding us, and empowering us as we love like Jesus here on earth. This is how Christ lives in us. Though He is seated at the right hand of the Father, His Spirit dwells within our hearts as believers while we live our everyday lives! This is how it's possible for you and me to no longer live, but for Christ to be alive within us, because the life we live in the flesh we live full of the Spirit by faith in Jesus (Galatians 2:20).

It is the Holy Spirit who helps us see every person we meet as our neighbor. It is through the Holy Spirit that we bear the fruit of love toward people even when they are giving us so many reasons to pass them by. He gives us a new nature, a new perspective, a new way of seeing people. The encounters we have with people every day are middle moments to either choose love or our own comfort zones, and by walking in step with the Spirit, we are compelled to choose what's most important.

8

When They Like You

*The man that takes up religion for the world will
throw away religion for the world.*

—John Bunyan

We wake up and, first things first, we have to check our phone.
It's as though seeing who emailed, who texted us back, who liked
or hopefully even commented on our most recent post is urgent.
Before our feet have even touched the floor, our minds are consumed with what people think about us, wanting them to approve.

In our conversations with people, sometimes even with our
own friends, we filter our words and expressions through a deep
desire to be accepted. It feels good to be liked. Though nothing is
wrong with this by itself, it has the potential to be problematic
when our confidence depends on the approval of others. How we
think, what we say, where we go, and even what we wear is easily
filtered through the question, "Will other people like it?" with-

out us even realizing. To be liked is comforting, but living out of
a need to be liked doesn't deliver the joy it promises to bring.

**To be liked is comforting, but living out of a
need to be liked doesn't deliver the joy it
promises to bring.**

THE MAJORITY

In 1951, Solomon Asch conducted a famous conformity experiment. He brought groups of eight men into his lab, where they
were shown three lines drawn at various lengths and a target line.
Each person was asked to identify which of the three lines
matched the target line. The answer was obvious each time, but
as the experiment progressed, there was a catch. Seven of the
eight subjects in the room were actors who had been instructed
to unanimously choose the incorrect answer. The remaining individual in the group was unaware of their strategy. So when it
was time for him to select which line was most like the target
line, he was thrown off seeing that his peers were choosing differently from what he saw to be accurate. In this paradigm, he was
faced with the decision to either go with what was clearly correct
or go with what everyone else was picking.

This "unanimous" version of the test was given twelve different times, and the results are worth contemplating. Asch found

that out of the twelve trials, 74 percent of the participants chose to go along with the majority at least once, even though the majority was plainly wrong. After the results came in, the participants were invited to share what their thought process was as they made their decision in the experiment. Most of them admitted that "they did not really believe their conforming answers, but had gone along with the group for fear of being ridiculed or thought 'peculiar.'"[1]

When we are standing in the middle of a decision, it is typical for us to heavily consider what people will think of the route we choose. Most often, our desire to be liked and not be "thought peculiar" matters more to us than doing what we know to be right. So we follow the majority. Our fear of what people will think and our love for the comfort of fitting in sways us with great force. As we saw in Asch's research, those who knew the right answer still chose the wrong one so they could avoid ridicule. Being wrong was worth being liked. In the same way, many of us know deep in our hearts that going with God is best, and yet we conform to what everyone else is doing to be accepted.

RESPONDING TO PRAISE

There is a story in Scripture about two men named Paul and Barnabas. They had been traveling together for quite some time, going from city to city telling people about Jesus. Many people in these cities were giving their lives to Christ, and what God was doing was beautiful. In Acts 14, Paul and Barnabas made their way to a city known as Lystra. While Paul was speaking there one day, he locked eyes with a man who was unable to walk and had been that way since birth. By discernment through the Holy Spirit, Paul knew that this man had faith, so he told the man to get up and walk. And by God's power, the man got up, completely healed!

The people of Lystra who witnessed this were utterly amazed at what had just happened. They were so amazed, in fact, that they were convinced Paul and Barnabas were actual gods. The people said, "The gods have come down to us in human form!" (Acts 14:11, NIV). They called Paul "Hermes," and Barnabas "Zeus."

Though this initially sounds like a farfetched reaction, it is important we know what shaped their religious perspective and led them to respond this way. A legend held that long ago Zeus and Hermes visited the city of Lystra disguised as mortals. They went to a thousand homes looking for lodging, but not a single person welcomed them. Making their way to an elderly couple who lived in a poor cottage, they were greeted and treated with great hospitality. The gods responded by honoring the elderly couple but destroying the homes of all the people who rejected them. With this legend deeply rooted in the history of Lystra, and after witnessing Paul perform the miracle for the lame man, it seems the people were convinced this had to be the gods returning. So the priest of Zeus went to the temple to retrieve bulls and wreaths so that sacrifices could be offered to them. The villagers didn't want to upset the gods a second time around, so they were extravagant in ensuring that Paul and Barnabas felt most welcomed.

When Paul and Barnabas heard what the people were believing and that they were en route to offer sacrifices to them, the two men tore their robes, rushed to the crowd, and said, "Friends, why are you doing this? We too are only human, like you. We are bringing you good news, telling you to turn from these worthless things to the living God" (Acts 14:15, NIV). But Scripture says that after Paul and Barnabas poured out their hearts to correct the people, "they scarcely restrained the people from offering sacrifice to them" (Acts 14:18).

If Paul and Barnabas wanted to, they could have gone right along with the people, agreeing with them, pretending to be who they weren't just so they could have the attention. Or, they easily could have kept quiet, allowing the people to keep believing that they were gods, justifying their silence as a means of creating an opportunity for the gospel to be shared.

Would we be as quick as Paul and Barnabas to take the attention off ourselves if people were honoring us erroneously? Would we rush to correct the majority's understanding, knowing that would mean their opinion of us would change? It is easy to believe that we would, but in our everyday moments, giving glory to God rather than taking it for ourselves is not our instinctive reaction.

Proverbs 27:21 says, "A man is tested by his praise." Receiving attention and praise has a way of exposing us, making known what has been there all along. How we respond to the praise of people sheds light on the honest motive for our actions. Paul's and Barnabas's true hearts were exposed when they stood in the middle moment of deciding how to respond to the people. They knew only God, the One True God, deserved to be worshipped.

Their motivation for going to Lystra was not to be praised by people, hence the reason their response was so immediate and passionate. Their motivation was the love of Christ. Their motivation was the gospel. Their motivation was God's approval, and this shaped their perspective of what the people thought about them.

OUR NEED FOR CONNECTION LEFT EMPTY IN OUR STRIVING TO BE LIKED

The opinions of people stop being our end-all when we start seeing God's glory as more important than having the majority think a certain way about us. Though we aren't seeking affirmation to the point of people thinking we are gods and offering sacrifices to us, the desire for acclaim has not faded away. Nowadays, this behavior disguises itself in our "worship" of celebrities and influencers—individuals we place upon pedestals—as we scroll for hours to watch their content, or stand in lines for hours and spend thousands of dollars to see them. We almost have a subconscious expectation for celebrities to be more than human.

Whether we're famous or not, most of us would think it is flattering to hear that people approve of us. Our excitement to be accepted points to the beautiful God-given desire in us for connection and belonging. When we try to satisfy this desire for connection by striving for the approval of others, we sell ourselves short and live a life that is conformed and covered up. Unlike Paul and Barnabas, when we need to be liked we start to go along with what everyone thinks so we can maintain a certain image in the eyes of many, just so we can belong. In doing so, we become someone we were never meant to be. In our desperation to be liked, we end up becoming someone we don't even like ourselves. We rob ourselves of the true connection we were made for because we are trying to become everything to everyone. Relationships can't go beyond surface level when we persist in covering up and conforming for the purpose of approval.

When we try to satisfy this desire for connection by striving for the approval of others, we start living a life that is conformed and covered up.

Though this hustle is driving us crazy, we are being encouraged to live this way. The world tells us that if more people agree with us, certain people like us, and other groups invite us in, then we can have peace. But the peace that the world offers is like cotton candy, tasting sweet for a moment but lasting just about that long: a moment. And then the cycle of exhaustion continues as we strive for more affirmation, more attention, and more approval. That downward spiral sometimes satisfies the hunger of our ego, but it never satisfies the hunger for connection in our souls. None of us want to chase those moments for all of our days just to look up and not recognize the person in the mirror because we were tirelessly working to be who we thought everyone wanted us to be. We are weary from living compelled by the approval of others because it is a burden that God never designed us to carry. Living for the Lord's approval can feel lonely at times, but living for the majority guarantees a life of loneliness. Yet we cannot live for both. We are living for one or the other.

THE NEED TO BE LIKED
CREATES A NEED TO BE SEEN

Our need for approval from others not only affects us in our general day-to-day, but it also affects the way we practice spiritual disciplines and serve in our local churches. Posting about our time in prayer has become a Christian cultural norm. Many of us are serving our congregation and then sharing about all the titles and responsibilities we have, thinking it will sound impressive to those who hear. For some, being a Christian has become more of a social tag than a sacrificing of self.

In Matthew 6, Jesus was teaching His disciples about giving, praying, and fasting. He stressed the importance of not doing those things in a manner so as to intentionally bring attention to themselves. These instructions Jesus gave contradicted the example being set by the religious leaders at the time—not because of what they were doing, but because of why they were doing it.

To many people it probably seemed like the religious leaders' relationship with God was thriving. But just because their actions took on a form of godliness doesn't mean that they had pure motives. In Jesus's conversation with His disciples, He referred to the religious leaders as "hypocrites" (Matthew 6:2). Another word for this is "actors." They were pretending. Their actions communicated love for God, but their motives were driven by praise from people. Jesus said that they would sound a trumpet in the synagogues and in the streets as they gave to the needy. They would stand out at street corners and in the synagogues while praying so that others would see them. They would disfigure their faces, looking gloomy and agonized out in public so people would take note of them and know they were fasting. They were doing all the correct spiritual things, if you will, but their actions were abhorrent because there was no love for God or people in what they did. The only love in their actions was love for themselves.

The purpose of giving is to serve people, to bless them, and to show them who God is. The purpose of praying and fasting is to draw near to God, intercede on behalf of others, and put away distractions so we can set our eyes on the Father. The religious leaders were missing all of this. While the attention might have felt nice in the moment, who knows the depth of intimacy with God those leaders were robbing themselves of—intimacy that God longed to have with them? In the same way, so many of us are missing a deeper friendship with God because spiritual disciplines and good deeds are motivated by what people will think instead of being compelled by love for Him. Jesus said that those who give and pray and fast for the purpose of getting people's attention "have received all the reward they will ever get" (Matthew 6:2, NLT). In other words, the approval from people that motivated the religious leaders' actions in the first place would be the extent of their satisfaction.

Making decisions for recognition from others is not a new

concept, either. Being loud about what we do might not look the way it did a couple thousand years ago, but in today's culture, we can bring hundreds, if not thousands, of people into the loop on what we are doing in just a matter of seconds. And not too long after that we are notified with an overflow of views, likes, and comments. There are algorithms we are working hard to learn with the hopes of gaining more followers so that more people can see what we share, hear what we say, and be further informed on how we live our life. I am not saying these spaces are bad or that we need to shy away from them. They are spaces to leverage for the glory of God and not our own. In order to do this, though, the secret motive of our hearts cannot be the approval of people. If our end goal in all of this—in serving, in sharing, in praying, in fasting—is simply for more people to know our name and like who we are, then we, like the religious leaders, are missing the whole point.

CHOOSING SECRECY

In contrast to the actions of the religious leaders, Jesus told His disciples to give and pray and fast in secret. Now, this is not for the purpose of avoiding people or to make us afraid of people seeing us do good things. Being seen or unseen is not the point here. What Jesus is getting at is the posture of our hearts as we do what we do. He was saying that our motive in doing good deeds should be purely to love God and love people—not to gain the attention of others.

When we practice spiritual disciplines and faithfully serve

those around us, let's not do it so other people will take note of us, holding us in high regard. Rather, let us do it for the individual concerned. Let's do it for the benefit of the person we are serving. If we are recognized, all glory goes to God, and if we aren't noticed for even a moment, all glory still goes to God. Let's do it for God, knowing that our Father who sees what is done in secret will bring a greater reward than any amount of praise could ever supply. Jesus is inviting us to evaluate our motives, maybe now more than ever before with attention being easier to get than it has ever been. Are we motivated by approval and attention from people, or are we motivated by the approval of God? Are we receiving the best we are going to get from a few moments of applause, or is the secret place of our hearts consumed with a desire to give all praise to God?

YOUR CHOICE GOES BEYOND YOU

A few years after Solomon Asch's study on the influence of social pressure, he decided to conduct another experiment. In 1956, he introduced a different dynamic to the group. Asch wanted to see how much the inclination to conform would shift, if it would at all, by bringing in an individual who would intentionally go against what the majority collectively decided. Sorting through the results, he discovered that when just one person chose to differ from the majority, the success of conformity decreased by as much as 80 percent. By one person choosing to be set apart, other people felt they had permission to go against the grain too.

When we stop living like our purpose is to fit in and start living out our faith with boldness, we don't just help ourselves. Whether we see it in the moment or not, we are helping others have the confidence to give all glory to God too. Paul and Barnabas didn't allow the majority to pull them into conformity. They refused to receive praise that was not theirs to take. Instead of being consumed with worry about whether they were liked, they were consumed with the love of Jesus. That was what drove them, and their boldness carried far beyond that middle moment. Their boldness has made its way to you and me today, encouraging us to do likewise.

When people praise us, may the secret place of our hearts be found humbled as we give all glory to God. Even when the majority is seeking attention for themselves, may we be found directing attention to the God who is worthy of all the praise. Instead of living for a need to be temporarily liked, may we live from the secure place of knowing we are already unconditionally loved. And from this place, may we live compelled to love others, with no other agenda found in our motive.

Instead of living for a need to be temporarily liked, may we live from the secure place of knowing we are already unconditionally loved. And from this place, may we live compelled to love others, with no other agenda found in our motive.

Whether on a public platform, across our campus, in our workplace, or in the four walls of our home—let's be all about Him. Whether seen or unseen, let's desire for Him to become greater and ourselves to become less (John 3:30). Let's conduct ourselves in a manner worthy of the gospel of Christ (Philippians 1:27). Let's "consider [our] life worth nothing to [us because our] only aim is to finish the race and complete the task the Lord Jesus has given [us]—the task of testifying to the good news of God's grace" (Acts 20:24, NIV). Let's live for God's approval, whether people like us, or they don't.

9

And When They Don't

Never mind man's frown if God smiles.
—CATHERINE BOOTH

The jokes weren't funny. They felt weighty. The cruel comments glared at me through the screen. My heart ached. My stomach twisted in knots.

Greater depths of my desire to please people became exposed when people started publicly mocking me for my faith. What started out as comments making fun of my smile and my joy as I sat in the bleachers later turned into satirical videos made of my love for Jesus. I didn't know what a meme was until I became one. Each stranger's opinion of my voice, my smile, and my faith had a volume dial, and I fought to keep that volume on low. Fear reacted like Velcro, and it seemed like I was daily having to resist its determination to stick to me. Even though I knew timidity was not the spirit God had given me, it lurked outside my door, and it was a moment-by-moment decision not to let it take residence in my mind (2 Timothy 1:7).

People have opinions and people express their thoughts, kind or unkind. This is just reality. But being afraid of others' opinions does not have to be our reality. Being crippled by fear is a choice that we all get to make with each new day. If we aren't careful, fear of what people think can seep into every crevice of our lives. Perhaps, if we allow the opinions of others to have too much power over us, we will look up one day to realize we never lived the life we were made for because we were so afraid of what others thought.

We might find that we didn't share a smile or a compliment because we were afraid someone would think we were weird. Maybe we discover that we shied away from initiating conversations about Jesus because being made fun of was too hard to bear. If we live letting fear call the shots, we very well could look up to discover that we compromised on our values, disregarded the voice of God, and went along with everything others did because we were convinced that was what it took to be liked. Grimacing at the mere thought of being unfollowed and having our thoughts clouded with the fear of being canceled, we may even choose to never go public about our faith. Fearing the opinions of others has a way of deterring us from walking along the path we were made to walk. It has a way of regularly deciding which path we take in our middle moments.

In his poem "The Road Not Taken," Robert Frost wrote, "Two roads diverged in a wood, and I—I took the one less traveled by, and that has made all the difference."[1] Many times, the decisions in our lives that make all the difference are the ones that require us to let go of the fear of what others think, and to step forward even when doing so is controversial, misunderstood, or just plain unconventional. I have come to find that some of my best decisions were made when I was okay that people might not approve of me. Committing to boldly live out my faith and be who God uniquely made me to be has required a willingness to take the road less traveled.

Committing to boldly live out my faith and be who God uniquely made me to be has required a willingness to take the road less traveled.

RESPONDING TO THE HATE

Remember the story in Acts 14 about Paul and Barnabas, who were believed to be gods by the people of Lystra? Well, we haven't finished the story. We left off at the part where the people praised these two men, worshipped them in fact, and had sacrifices on the way to be offered to them.

After Paul and Barnabas rushed to point the people to God instead, some Jews from Antioch and Iconium made their way into the city. Antioch and Iconium were the places Paul and Barnabas had visited prior to coming to Lystra, and so the Jews who came onto the scene were not unaware of who these two guys were. More than likely, the Jews who came to Lystra were driven by jealousy to go against what Paul and Barnabas were saying because they didn't like the message they shared, and they didn't like how much attention they were getting. With this agenda, the Jews began to spread word that the people should not listen to Paul and Barnabas. They persuaded the people of Lystra to stop listening, and went so far as to convince them to stone Paul and drag him out of the city!

The same people who were praising Paul and proclaiming him to be a god in one moment were talked into stoning him and dragging him out of the city in the next. They went from welcoming him to acting as though they wished he had never entered their city. They went from claiming he was a god to being convinced he wasn't worth another second of their attention. Paul had their applause and approval in its fullness, and with the snap of a finger and a couple words of condemnation from a few, he was shunned.

The extreme fickleness of this crowd teaches us that the opinions of people are not a steady, sure ground to walk on. One day we might be told that we are fun to hang out with, only to find ourselves rejected the next day. If we are choosing to center our identity in approval, we are setting ourselves up for a life of insecurity.

Many of us are going about our days as though the opinions of people have a stronger grip on us than the Word of God does. We have our shoulders slouched, our head held low, and our heart weighed down in discouragement because we are holding on tightly to the hurtful words people have spoken. We often posture in an anxiety-ridden state, terrified of the inescapable reality that there will be people who don't like us.

We might have quite a few Scripture verses memorized, but many of us have yet to believe God's words and let them be our means of discernment in how we respond to the lies we are hearing. We cannot walk in the authority, freedom, and life change that Scripture gives if all we are doing is merely memorizing some of the popular Bible verses. Remember, simply recalling Scripture as I sat in the bleachers wasn't what gave me the courage to live compelled in that middle moment. It was, with the help of the Holy Spirit, actually trusting the words I had memorized to be true that gave me strength. We must know what God says, believe His promises, and put His words into action, or the opinions of people will continue to have a greater grip on us than the Word of God does in our middle moments. We won't walk in the authority of the truth if we don't believe God's Word to be true.

Paul had an opportunity. He could either cower down in fear of the people or he could remain confident in God even though he was in a scary situation. It is significant that Paul and Barnabas tore their clothes in dismay when finding out that the people of Lystra were intent on worshipping them, because they did no such thing when Paul's life was on the line for preaching about Christ.

The early-eighteenth-century author and pastor Matthew Henry wrote of Paul and Barnabas in his commentary:

We do not find that they rent their clothes when the people vilified them, and spoke of stoning them; they could bear this without disturbance: but when they deified them, and spoke of worshipping them, they could not bear it, but rent their clothes, as being more concerned for God's honor than their own.[2]

Being ridiculed for their faith seems to have been something they expected, but to take any glory from God instantly demanded a response. The treasure of their hearts was revealed in this moment. God's glory and honor were their deepest desire. The possibility of being killed for their faith was nothing compared with the experience of credit being given to them that was due to God alone.

Scripture says that as the disciples gathered around Paul after he had been dragged out of the city, he proceeded to get up and go back into the very same city that had just tried to kill him for what he was preaching. This action alone communicates that Paul was not living for himself. It didn't matter that these people wanted to kill him. It didn't matter that he had just been dragged out of the city. It didn't matter that there were people strategically contradicting the message he preached. It didn't matter because he was compelled. Nothing was stopping him from proclaiming the gospel because he was moved by the love of Christ. After this, Scripture says:

On the next day he went on with Barnabas to Derbe. When they had preached the gospel to that city and had made many disciples, they returned to Lystra and to Iconium and to Antioch, strengthening the souls of the disciples, encouraging them to continue in the faith, and saying that through many tribulations we must enter the kingdom of God. (Acts 14:20–22)

How we respond to the praise or the disapproval of people reveals where our confidence truly rests.

Paul not only went back into Lystra, but he also strengthened the disciples in that city and encouraged them to keep going in their faith. He could have ruminated on the valid reasons he had to be afraid that the people would persist in persecuting him. Out of this fear, he could have left the believers who were still in Lystra, ignoring opportunities for discipleship there. He could have sulked in the self-pity of rejection, even beginning to debate whether he should continue to the next city. If so many people in Lystra wanted him dead, he could have concluded that entering the next town wasn't worth it.

Often, this is how our thought process goes. The feeling of defeat that comes from the disapproval of one person can discourage us from living unashamed of the gospel. Meanwhile, we probably don't even realize that people are also encouraged by our faithfulness. Yes, Paul was persecuted in Lystra. But let's not overlook that there were also people who gave their life to Jesus and were equipped with the truth in that city! We must not grow weary in doing good and we must not assume that God is not working if we are experiencing hardship. God is always working. Knowing this spurs us on to boldly live out our faith in middle moments.

Paul did not neglect to revisit the city of Lystra out of concern about being stoned by so many people there. Rather, his perspective was one of faith in God. He knew that God was doing a good thing in that city, and he could not overlook the believers there who needed encouragement. He chose to go back. How could he do this? How was he not discouraged to the point of throwing in the towel and backing out? How did he have the strength to do that which seems impossible? People were giving him legitimate reasons to do so. The enemy was giving him some pretty strong arguments as to why he should stop right then and there. Yet he persisted in the mission of Jesus. He remained committed to the ancient paths. How?

Paul was able to move forward with endurance and encouragement because he saw the situation from a perspective of eternity. His focus was on a picture much grander than the opinions of people in front of him. The approval of people was not his filter for decision making. His filter was the purpose to which God had called him. He was compelled to please God. His aim was to bring glory to God. His goal upon entering Lystra was to care for the hearts of the people there by sharing the gospel with them and making disciples of those who had come to faith in Jesus. This was his mission even if it meant that people rejected him along the way. This was the same man who wrote, "For am I now seeking the approval of man, or of God? Or am I trying to please man? If I were still trying to please man, I would not be a servant of Christ" (Galatians 1:10).

Paul knew that following God with all his heart and living in obedience to Him meant that hardships would come. He knew that any suffering he faced was worth honoring the God who gave him eternal life. All that mattered to him was expressing his faith in love. Nothing—not jealous people, not rejection, and not even physical pain from persecution—could make him "throw away [his] confidence" (Hebrews 10:35).

CONFUSION FROM COMMENTS

If the opinions of people are where we turn to learn about who we are and the life we need to be living, we will find ourselves chasing every comment people vocalize in person and type on a screen, only to still be confused about who we are and where we are going. This is universal. No matter who we are, or how likable we may be, living off the approval of people is a roller coaster for anyone.

Singer and songwriter Taylor Swift shared in an interview that people have told her:

> Be new to us, be young to us—but only in a new way and only the way we want. Reinvent yourself, but only in a way that we find to be equally comforting and a challenge for you. Live out a narrative that we find interesting enough to entertain us, but not so crazy that it makes us uncomfortable.[3]

Taylor Swift has millions of people across the globe who adore her, and yet the approval she receives from the majority is still conditional on her living up to what they want. Believing one's value is based on meeting these expectations would fatigue anyone's soul.

Looking at my own life, I know I would grow weary if I took to heart what every person said about me. People have told me that they love me, and people have told me that they hate me. I have read comments saying how gorgeous I am and others saying how hideous I am, as they specifically address the reasons why. People have expressed to me that my faith in Christ is make-believe, while others have expressed how encouraged they are by my faith. My phone has lit up to notify me that people think my smile is contagious. On that very same day, I have been informed that people think my joy is fake and my smile is cringey. People have gone out of their way to tell me how calming and peaceful my voice is, and others have let me know they don't like the way I talk, that I sound like a baby to them.

If approval is what I am chasing, I would have a life ahead of me that is crammed with headaches and confusion. If my life's goal were to try to change the minds of the many people who made so many cruel comments about me, it would be like running on a treadmill. I would spend an unspeakable amount of time exerting all my energy and end up going nowhere. I'd waste precious time, and no matter how hard I tried, on the day I die there would still be people who like me and there would still be people who don't.

So at the end of the day, when we are striving to gain the approval of people, how are we defining success? When would we feel we have "arrived"? Since there will always be someone who doesn't like us, will we continue committing to a life of strife while still always feeling like we have failed? Surely there is a better way to live.

To steady and strengthen ourselves when hearing the threats and opinions and mockery against us, we must rely on the Word of God like we rely on our bed to support us when we go to sleep each night—full of trust that we will be held up and comforted no matter what. By depending on what He says with everything we have, we will be able to have a soul at rest whether a thousand comments or just a single comment is sent our way. His Word reminds us: "Do not conform to the pattern of this world, but be transformed by the renewing of your mind. Then you will be able to test and approve what God's will is—his good, pleasing and perfect will" (Romans 12:2, NIV). His Word enlightens our eyes so we can see and focus on what is worth our attention (Psalm 19:8). "His faithful promises are [our] armor and protection" from the lies of the evil one (Psalm 91:4, NLT).

THE RIPPLE EFFECT OF LIVING AFRAID

Living in fear of what people think doesn't only sap our strength, but it also holds us back from loving others freely. We cannot be completely focused on serving God and investing in the lives of people when we are all-consumed with worry about whether people approve of us or not. Paul said in 1 Corinthians 13:5 that love "is not self-seeking" (NIV). Isn't that what fearing the thoughts of people really is—an unhealthy focus on ourselves? When we are fearful of what people think of us, we are not able to think about how we can serve them because we are completely overwhelmed with fear about how we are being seen and what they might be thinking of us.

I'm reminded of a story from when my husband and I moved from our college town back to Arkansas one summer. I was ecstatic to meet my neighbors. I thought baking cookies for them would be a sweet and simple way to reach out and share the love of Christ. Well, Christmastime rolled around, and I had yet to bake a single cookie for a single person. I had let months go by without actually baking cookies and going to people's houses because I was so afraid of what the people on the other side of the door would think. What if I didn't have the right words for the perfect conversation and would therefore make the interaction feel awkward? So instead, I put off something that meant so much to me because of the fear of what someone might or might not think about me.

During those six months, I prayed for opportunities to connect with people in the neighborhood. Over and over again as I prayed, the thought to bake cookies and take them to my neighbors would resurface. Still, I did nothing.

How often do we pray for God to guide us and show us opportunities to bless people? And when He answers those prayers, how often do we turn down or fail to recognize those opportunities because fear is clouding our vision and fueling our excuse-filled responses? I wasn't lacking opportunities in my neighborhood or guidance from the Lord. Rather, because I was carrying with me an abundance of fear, I was lacking faithful action.

Sometimes when we think of God calling us to be obedient and share who He is with others, we believe it is going to be something that *appears* significant, like moving overseas, speaking to thousands, or starting a nonprofit. These could be things He calls us to do, which is amazing! But it's harder to believe that the unseen, day-to-day-life moments are significant too. Sometimes it is more difficult for us to have the perspective that mundane moments are opportunities to magnify Christ just as much as the grander moments.

God does not view significance the way we do. What is most significant to Him is not the extravagance of an act, but rather when we abide in Him and walk in obedience to His voice, in moments big or small. When we begin to have a perspective of significance the way God does, we will begin to take note of the many middle moments that consume our everyday. We will begin to see grocery runs as a chance to meet and bless people. We will begin to heed the moments in the gym to encourage people and share the gospel with them. We will begin to see the value and importance of the time we spend with our kids in the four walls of our home. We will begin to take note of the ministry opportunities just outside our front door in our very own neighborhoods. All these moments that occupy the hours of our days are middle moments to capitalize on through living compelled by the love of Christ. The significance of what we do is not based on the place or the title or how many people know about it. The significance of what we do is based on our obedience to the amazing God who has called us to do it.

I finally began to realize that I had been overcomplicating an act of kindness. That simple act of generosity was going to require that I step out of my comfort zone and out of my front door! I knew that if I waited for the fear to go away before I took cookies to my neighbors, then I might never put action behind this thought.

Fear has a way of keeping us so focused on ourselves and all the things that could possibly go wrong that we can convince ourselves to turn our focus away from Jesus and never take a step of faith. Living for the approval of people is a "weight" that bears down on us, hindering us from taking action in the right direction. These weights and "sin which clings so closely" (Hebrews 12:1) distract us from where we were made to fix our gaze. Scripture tells us to "run with endurance the race that is set before us, looking to Jesus" (Hebrews 12:1–2). This verb "looking" in the Greek means having an undistracted gaze on one thing, and "suggests the impossibility of looking in two directions at once."[4]

Jesus alone is worthy of our gaze because He is "the founder and perfecter of our faith" (Hebrews 12:2). Our faith is built on Him. He is the one who completed the redemptive work of making a way for us to have a genuine relationship with God by "endur[ing] the cross, despising the shame, and is [now] seated at the right hand of God" (Hebrews 12:2). By fixing our gaze on who Jesus is, we can confidently be who He made us to be—free, bold, and compelled by love.

By fixing our gaze on who Jesus is, we can confidently be who He made us to be—free, bold, and compelled by love.

WHAT OTHERS REALLY THINK OF YOU

How often do we turn down the dial of our excitement, our curiosity, and our love because we have assumed the possibility of rejection from other people? How often do we change our look and our lifestyle just to ensure that we aren't rocking the boat and causing disapproval from anyone? The answer is *a lot*! And what's even crazier is that more often than not, people aren't thinking twice about what we believe is at the forefront of their minds. "Studies show that we consistently overestimate how much, and how badly, others think about our failings. An unfortunate consequence of this is that we are far more inhibited and far less spontaneous and joyful than we could be."[5]

After wrestling with this fear and being encouraged by the Holy Spirit countless times, I decided that December that I couldn't hold back any longer. I went to the kitchen after church one Sunday afternoon, baked three batches of cookies, and put them in baggies. I wrote an encouraging note on each gift and took them to my neighbors, one knock on the door at a time.

As I started taking the focus off myself, I noticed the grip of fear loosen. I didn't want to stop. All I wanted to do was keep meeting people and giving them cookies. When I got back home, I was overflowing with joy—not because the people responded a certain way, but because I got to connect with them. I enjoyed being generous and telling each person how much I loved them. I was energized because I refused to let fear decide how I was going to spend my afternoon.

A couple of days later, our doorbell rang. One of our neighbors had stopped by to give us a dessert. He told me that he had taken the cookies I had given him to his workplace and shared them with his colleagues. This connection was only a few steps away, just across the street, but it had felt like it had been miles away for months because of fear.

How many opportunities to boldly live out our faith feel out of reach because of fear, but are actually just a few steps away? I have not forgotten the feeling of joy and confidence that overflowed from within me after God helped me take the focus off myself and put it onto how I could be obedient to Him in loving my neighbors. That energetic feeling of wanting to keep serving and encouraging was not because the sun was shining or because I had an extra cup of coffee that day. That feeling was pointing to the reality that we were made to walk in step with God, to be obedient to Him. We were made to invest in the lives of others. We were made to live a life of love!

How many opportunities to boldly live out
our faith feel out of reach because of fear,
but are actually just a few steps away?

The enemy schemes to keep us occupied with fear, to prevent us from living out and sharing our faith with others. Like a thief, he strategizes to steal our joy. He tries to rob our confidence, which flows from the inside out, and seeks to distract us from what really matters most.

When we stop fretting over what others might think of us and shift our focus to trusting in who God is, then God "will fill [us] with all joy and peace . . . so that by the power of the Holy Spirit [we] may abound in hope" (Romans 15:13). We can begin to live as if we truly believe that God has created us for something far too important to let fear keep us timid and self-focused. We can love God and love people with everything we have in us. We can live wholeheartedly. We can make the most of every breath in our lungs to show people how much they matter.

By walking in step with the Spirit, the love of Christ can seep into every crevice of our lives. We can share a smile and a compliment because we love people too much not to show them we care. We can keep opening up about what we truly believe, because it doesn't matter if anyone can cancel us. We can realize we don't mind being thought of as awkward, because the risk is worth taking if it means we can bring someone joy that refreshes their soul. We won't be driven by appeasing the expectations people have of our lives, because we can focus on being obedient to where God is leading. As God continues to give us the power to be confident in our faith, we can stop caring how many follow us or how many unfollow us, because nothing matters more than knowing and pleasing Him. We can look up one day and be filled with gratitude because we chose to live the life we were made to live.

We may not have to face being stoned and dragged out of a city, but no matter the form of disapproval we encounter, we can stand firm knowing that God's approval is worth more than the approval of any person. We also know that the souls of people He created are always worth loving. So there are two roads before us. One path is broad, and many take it, while the other is ancient and narrow, and very few find it (Matthew 7:13–14). I pray we take the road less traveled in our middle moments and discover that every step we take trusting in God makes all the difference.

10

Go When You Don't Know

Never be afraid to trust an unknown future to a known God.

—CORRIE TEN BOOM

She loved God and had committed to live for His glory when she was seventeen years old. No matter where she went, Amy Carmichael stewarded every opportunity she had to share the gospel, care for the poor and mistreated in the slums, and teach children about the Lord.

In 1892, at the age of twenty-four, Amy heard the Lord so clearly say, "Go ye," and she recalled what the Lord had spoken to His disciples: "Go ye into all the world and preach the gospel" (Mark 16:15, KJV). She felt as though God was telling her to go, but if she was to leave, so many dear relationships and responsibilities would be left behind. As far as what the future held, she had no clear answers. For starters, where would she even go? These unknowns kept her awake all throughout the night after hearing the Lord speak to her the day prior.

COMFORT ZONES

The unknown carries with it an element of fear and anxiety because it disrupts our feeling of control and takes us out of our comfort zone. According to psychiatrist Dr. Abigail Brenner, a comfort zone "is a psychological/emotional/behavior construct that defines the routine of our daily life [that] implies familiarity, safety, and security."[1]

We often equate certainty with safety. A lack of clarity on what is around the corner can easily cause our hearts and minds to quicken in a desperate desire to find steadiness, to regain a sense of control. We all, to some degree, innately love what is calculable and therefore dodge ambiguity when we can.

That said, there are benefits to having recognizable things in our lives. The comforting smell of walking into our own home after being away for a while and the familiar embrace from a loved one after a hard day are true gifts. Even when we work on tasks we are good at and are accustomed to, confidence comes more naturally because there is knowledge, comfort, and ease with what we are doing.

Though there are many beauties to the predictable parts of our lives, there is also incredible growth to be discovered on the other side of our willingness to go where there are paths not yet walked. Amy Carmichael learned this firsthand.

Amy went back and forth in her mind as she counted the cost of what following God's lead would mean. To submit to His will meant acknowledging that He was in control and she was not.

She had plans to stay in England longer, so would this mean she had to let that go?

After wrestling all night, she got up the next morning certain about one thing: God was worthy of her "yes," whatever the sacrifice. After informing her closest people of the journey she knew God was leading her to embark on, she considered leaving for China. She had some mutual connections with mission work being done there, so she thought that could be the place God wanted her to go.

She applied to serve with the China Inland Mission, having been accepted as a missionary, and even acquired an entirely new wardrobe to appropriately dress in China. She was learning the language and got to the point that she was literally waiting on a few more women to arrive at the China Inland Mission house before leaving.

Anyone would say things were falling into place without a hitch—until it came time for the results of her physical. It turns out that because of the work she had done with women in the slums of Belfast, her health was not in the best condition. In fact, it was bad enough for the doctor to reject her ability to travel to China. Just like that, Amy, with her tin sea chest, went back home. What had appeared to be falling into place seemed to completely dissolve in that one conversation.

Confused and probably feeling like she was right back where she started, Amy still didn't know where God was leading her. After everything had appeared to be lining up so well, she likely wondered why it fell through.

One of the ways we try to keep hold of control when following God into the unknown is that we place expectations on what God has spoken—expectations He never gave. When God tells us to go somewhere or places a vision on our heart, we often fill in the blanks for how we think He will work out certain details. We assume we will see His word come to pass within a certain time and in a specific way that makes the most sense to our own understanding. Therefore, we tirelessly aim at and wait with anticipation for our idea of what God meant, but we then find ourselves doubtful and disappointed when things aren't coming together as we expected.

Instead of holding such a tight grip on how we think God is supposed to carry out His plans, may we trust that even when circumstances aren't looking the way we think they should, God is faithful to see His promises through. He is never caught off guard by what we perceive to be plans falling through, because His plans never fall through.

Though Amy didn't quite know why China wasn't working out, she was certain that God was telling her to "go." Sitting in the balance of waiting for the unknown to become a bit clearer, Amy stood by readily. She waited not for a day, not even for another week. It wasn't until another four months passed by that Amy felt God was calling her to Japan. Though she had never been there and had never met anyone who lived there, she made plans to go. This couldn't have been easy, to have so little information about what the future held, and still proceed to go all in.

We must not wait for the next ten steps to be made known to us before walking in faith. If so, we wouldn't be walking by faith, but by our comfort of feeling in control. Those who live compelled by the love of Christ live by God's Word, which is a lamp for their feet and a light on their path (Psalm 119:105). They live by following Him step by step, even when that means they know their next step and nothing further.

RIGHT HERE, RIGHT NOW

Full commitment to following God's lead doesn't purge the heavy emotions that come with stepping into the unknown. Tears filled Amy's eyes as she had to greet the moment of saying farewell to the people she loved so dearly in England.

While out at sea, she could have kept to herself, worrying about her family she had left behind and the unknowns waiting ahead. Instead, within a week she helped organize Bible studies and Sunday services for anyone who wanted to join. She chose to view her time onboard not as a trip to stressfully get through, but as an adventure that was packed full of opportunities to share the gospel. She didn't see the voyage as a basic means of getting to the place where she would begin to be faithful. No, *everywhere,* even in the middle of unanswered next steps, was the place to be faithful. Her faithfulness on the ship was just as notable as her faithfulness in the homes of Japan. Everywhere she went was her mission field. She might not have known much about where she was going, but she did know she was going to live compelled by the love of Christ everywhere along the way.

When we are standing in the middle of what we have known and what we don't know yet, it can be easy for us to miss the value of where our feet are. May we not be so concerned about the un-known that we miss what God is doing right where we are on the boat of the in-between. There are moments to capitalize on in our uncertainty, moments to see people and love them, moments to be faithful in what feels like the insignificant spaces. This is what it looks like to live compelled by the love of Christ as we walk by faith, not by sight (2 Corinthians 5:7).

> May we not be so concerned about the un-known that we miss what God is doing right where we are on the boat of the in-between.

If everything happening wasn't a whirlwind enough, the ship Amy was on made its way through a typhoon just before reaching land. She made it to Japan just as her rampant motion sickness finally steadied, only to feel quite lost and alone amid the unfa-miliar language around her. Taking in the complexities of what she was standing in, she began laughing, because what else was there to do in such a situation?

Following God into the unknown doesn't ensure ease and exact clarity at every turn. It invites us to experience a deepening of faith and cultivates in us the ability to sincerely laugh without fear of what is to come (Proverbs 31:25). The joy of the Lord su-persedes our circumstances, not based on our sense of control but on trusting the God who is with us (Proverbs 16:20). Like Amy laughing in a typhoon on the shores of Japan, so can we genuinely smile in the middle of the unknown by knowing God is worth being right beside no matter where following Him takes us.

WALK BY FAITH

Through God's provision, Amy met people, found a place to stay, and for fifteen months faithfully served those in Japan. She shared the gospel and saw many put their faith in Jesus. Within that short period of time, her health eventually declined to such a degree that she had to leave Hirose, Japan, and return to England.

But even being back in the place that had originally been hard to leave, she was unsettled. She knew there was mission work still to be done and that her part in it was not finished. Exactly what her part was, though, she wasn't quite sure. In November 1895, she received a letter from a friend who worked in Bangalore, India, informing her that the climate there was fitting for her health conditions. Her friend invited Amy to come and work alongside her in a hospital there.

And so, with her hands wide open in complete surrender to God, at twenty-seven years old, Amy purchased a one-way ticket to southern India. For the last time, upon boarding the ship, she waved goodbye to her beloved friends in England whom she would never see again. Not knowing all that was set before her, she knew God was calling her to India, and she would eventually discover that India was going to be the place where she would serve God for the rest of her life.

Amy Carmichael went to India having been invited to serve in a hospital, yet ended up founding what is known as the Dohnavur Mission Orphanage. Through this ministry, she rescued babies and children from temple prostitution. Upon rescuing them, she taught them about Christ, and brought them up in love and truth. These children grew to call her "Amma"—"mother."

Time and time again we see Amy go by faith. She wasn't called to Japan or India by a message written in the clouds, but rather through the words of godly people around her and by seeking the Lord's prompting in prayer. Amy trusted that God would establish her steps (Proverbs 16:3).

One of the obstacles that often gets in the way of our following God into the unknown is fear that we will make a move outside of God's will. Many of us think that we control whether His plan is fulfilled in our lives. By thinking this way, we live paralyzed in fear, convinced that with one wrong move, we could ruin God's plan. Rather than committing our ways to God and stepping out in faith, we decide to stay put and not go anywhere at all. Everything feels too risky. The mere idea of messing up is too great a burden to bear. Amy Carmichael, too, could have been so afraid of choosing the wrong place to go that she remained in England. Imagine if she had been so afraid of making the wrong move that she just stayed where she was. Yet people who didn't know Christ, and children held captive in temple prostitution, were waiting on the other side of her obedience to go.

When discerning where the Lord is leading, we can know that our faith in Him pleases Him (Hebrews 11:6). He honors the heart that is seeking to do His will and He doesn't leave us all alone to figure out His plan. Rather than standing still in our middle moments, afraid of making the wrong move, we seek the Lord in prayer, seek Him in His Word, surround ourselves with godly counsel, and as we go, trust that He is in control, His purpose cannot be thwarted (Job 42:2), and He is faithful to lead us on level ground (Psalm 143:10).

Walking into unfamiliar territory was a theme in Amy's life. She never knew exactly how long she was to stay in a particular place, or who all she was going to meet when she got there. From traveling overseas, to leaving loved ones behind, to facing ongoing illness, to getting rejected from where she thought she was supposed to go, to showing up in countries she had never been to for the purpose of serving people she had never met—unknowns were normal for her. She had an abundance of opportunities to quit. Giving the excuse that the unknown was too scary to navigate would have been understandable. In England she knew the lay of the land. She knew many familiar faces. She was comfortable. But her confidence in what she did know gave her the strength to walk the path of what she didn't. She did know for certain that she was to go in love for God and love for people (Matthew 28:19; Matthew 22:37–40).

LOOKING TO ETERNITY

Amy was not a unique case in being led to walk by faith and not by sight. All throughout the Scriptures, we see God call His people to follow Him into the unknown. It comes with the territory of living a life compelled by the love of Christ.

One particular man in the Bible who left us a great deal of lessons about releasing his need for control was Abraham. Well into Abraham's life, God met him and called him to leave everything he knew, for God had a new place to show him. This was no small ask because where Abraham lived was the place he and his family had been settled for many, many years. They had established their routines in that place and taken up residence there.

So Abraham had a decision to make. He had to choose if he was going to trust that God's way was better than his own. Scripture says that:

> By faith Abraham, when called to go to a place he would later receive as his inheritance, obeyed and went, even though he did not know where he was going. By faith he made his home in the promised land like a stranger in a foreign country; he lived in tents. (Hebrews 11:8–9, NIV)

It was not by knowing what his next season of life would look like that Abraham got unsettled to go with God. It was not by clinging to control that he made his home in a foreign country. It was by faith. Life did not become easy for Abraham once he decided to pack up everything he owned and lead his family into the unknown with God. It wouldn't be until much later that he would receive what God had promised him. Every day he had to make the choice to walk by faith. He didn't arrive in the land God led him to and immediately recognize the place and feel at home there. It was a foreign land. There wasn't a house ready for him when he arrived, either. He was a nomad, living in tent after tent. Every tent setup and tear-down was a constant reminder that Abraham was following God's lead, not his own.

How did Abraham do it? What was Abraham's motivation to go to a place, sight unseen? What kept him choosing God over and over again? With the unknowns that each day held, how did he step into them with such faith and endurance?

The author of Hebrews went on to say that Abraham "was looking forward to the city with foundations, whose architect and builder is God" (Hebrews 11:10, NIV). Abraham met the unknowns of living in tents, navigating a foreign land, and leaving everything he knew to follow God with confident knowledge of the hope to come. He was sure of eternity with God. And not only that, but he also knew eternity with God was his home. If anything, the tents were a picture of the reality that his time on earth was temporary. In fact, Scripture says he lived in a way that admitted he was a foreigner and stranger on Earth (Hebrews 11:13).

Amid so much that he did not know, Abraham did know that God was with him. He knew that his future forever home was with God. This gave his faith grit.

What kept Abraham going sounds awfully similar to what kept Amy Carmichael going. By setting their eyes on eternity, they had the strength to press on with purpose as each day came. The same hope anchored them even though they lived thousands of years apart.

Walking by faith is not just something that people in the Bible were called to do. Nor is following God into the unknown something set aside only for people we consider to be superheroes of the faith like Amy Carmichael. Walking by faith is the requirement of a disciple, a requirement for you and for me. Following God in complete surrender is vital to a life compelled by the love of Christ. We are called to follow God's lead even when there is great uncertainty in the journey. Because we know the territory of God's presence, we can walk confidently into the unknown territories of life.

Like Abraham, many of us are established in our routine. We have our own way of doing things. We are settled. We like how our life is looking, and we are comfortable in it. So hearing God call us to follow Him into the unknown can shake us up a bit, challenging our faith. We have desires for our life to look a certain way. Many of us long to get married, have children, live in a certain city, have a specific career—and we would prefer all of this to take place within a set time frame. We fear that totally abandoning our plans for a life with God will uproot what we have put in place and not end up as we hope. Maybe we are afraid God will let us down, thinking that the plans we have for our lives are better than God's plan for us. It is hard to go all in with God, knowing that could mean letting go of some dreams we have held so tightly for so long.

And God cares about the dreams we have for our lives. The deepest longings of our hearts matter to Him. It is not as though He steps in and changes all our plans just because He can. Rather, He has a good, purposeful, glorious plan for our lives, and sometimes the road map we have organized for ourselves is not the best. This is challenging to hear and believe because oftentimes what we want typically seems ideal to us.

I am not inviting you to throw away your hopes and dreams. In fact, I am inviting you to press into them. Only, do so with God. I am inviting you to trust God with the vision and plans you have on your heart, confident that He will establish your steps and lead you in paths of righteousness for His name's sake (Proverbs 16:9; Psalm 23:1). I am inviting you to take delight in God and discover that no matter how the plans of your life unfold, journeying with Him brings a contentment and fulfillment nothing else compares to. Not only does God have your heart in mind as He directs your path, but as He leads you, He also has the hearts of others on His mind. Following God into the unknown goes far beyond us. The impact made through our obedience is greater than our individual lives and stories. Amy's yes not only led to the salvation of souls in Belfast and Japan and India, but it also carried on to generations beyond her own as her "great-grandchildren" continue her ministry today. Abraham's yes led to the blessing of nations. Our yes to God will reach the souls of others for the glory of God "far more abundantly than all that we ask or think, according to the power at work within us" (Ephesians 3:20–21). Through our continual willingness to go with God, even with questions unanswered, we can know that God will do a mighty work throughout our homes, communities, nation, and world for the sake of the gospel.

Though there are many unknowns in walking by faith and not by sight, there is one thing we can know for sure: We no longer live for ourselves, but for Him who died for us and was raised

(2 Corinthians 5:15, CSB). The hope that anchored Abraham and Amy is the same hope that anchors us today. This is because that hope is Christ, who "is the same yesterday and today and forever" (Hebrews 13:8).

In our middle moments, we can walk into what we don't know by being secure in what we do know.

11

Go When It's Hard

The secret is Christ in me, not me in a different set of circumstances.

—Elisabeth Elliot

When we persist, we are choosing to stay the course so we can meet a desired goal. We all have persisted in something. If we have the goal of getting a promotion in our career, we persist in doing our work with excellence day in and day out. If we have the goal of making a sports team, we persist in practicing and working out and caring about our nutritional health so that we are best fit to securing a spot on the roster.

Thomas Edison had the goal of inventing the incandescent lightbulb, and so he persisted in a vast amount of research and tests. It is recorded that within a two-year span, Edison and his team "worked on at least three thousand different theories to develop an efficient incandescent lamp."[1] Even when Edison finally figured out how to build a light that worked, it only produced light for a few hours, and he was determined to put a light together that burned for a longer time. He stated, "Before I got through, I tested no fewer than six thousand vegetable growths, and ransacked the world for the most suitable filament material." This means that Edison and his team came across literally thousands of reasons to give up before getting where they wanted to be.

It is one thing to have a goal and persist in seeing it met. It is quite another to persevere in meeting our goal when we are faced with obstacles along the way. This is where our persistence is put to the test. One of the most insightful lessons we can learn from Edison is not what he invented, but rather his commitment to his goal despite the difficulties he encountered. As he put it, "Genius is one percent inspiration and ninety-nine percent perspiration." There will be times as we are aiming to accomplish our goal when we won't feel like continuing. There will be days we don't feel inspired. There will be moments when we want to quit because the path is hard to persist on. These are the moments when we must choose what it is we want more: the victory of meeting the goal set before us or the instant comfort of bowing out and taking the easier road.

This reality carries into our faith as well. To meet our goal of boldly living out our faith in middle moments, we persist in a personal relationship with Christ, growing in knowledge of Him and abiding in Him every day. We keep hiding His Word in our hearts, letting it dwell among us richly, filling us to the brim. We continue unconditionally loving people, not considering who is worth being our neighbor, but compelled by the love of Christ to be the best neighbor to everyone we meet. We persist in godliness to meet the goal of glorifying Christ with our lives. Paul wrote it best when he said, "I consider my life worth nothing to me; my only aim is to finish the race and complete the task the Lord Jesus has given me—the task of testifying to the good news of God's grace" (Acts 20:24, NIV). We live differently when we live persistent on the goal that the Lord Jesus has given to us.

ONE THING AFTER ANOTHER

In 1858, a young woman by the name of Sallie Holmes married her husband, Landrum, and just three weeks after the wedding bells rang they were selected by the International Mission Board to be missionaries in China. These two were unified in purpose. Their goal was to make disciples of all nations for the sake of Christ. They were burdened by the thought of the lost souls in China, and even though they were just a few weeks into marriage, going to China to serve as missionaries perfectly aligned with their goal. So they went.

Most women in their early twenties at that time were probably thinking about what they might do for work or how they would care for their home. Sallie's goal to share Jesus with those who had never heard about Him was not like the goals of those around her, but it was normal for a woman persistent in her faith. For someone completely sold out for Christ, there was no other way to live. Because Sallie's goal was to see people who didn't know Jesus come to know Him, she persisted in godliness, and her life looked different from most.

After leaving the shores of New York, Sallie and Landrum

traveled by ship for months—twenty-two weeks, to be exact—to reach Shanghai. Over the course of the next two years, they built relationships with people, learned the language, and had their daughter, Annie. In this regard many things were going wonderfully, but in other ways their road was a bit rocky.

During the time they were getting settled in Shanghai, society was unsettled not only in China but back in America as well. In China, an intense civil war was in full swing. It was the Taiping Rebellion, leading to the death of more than 20 million people. The unrest was also a specific challenge for Christian missionaries because the leader of the war was twisting the message of Scripture and making it his own. Therefore, the Christians interested in sharing the hope of Christ were coming into a uniquely difficult situation.

At the same time, the Civil War was breaking out in America. With most of Sallie's family living in Virginia (the South) and some of her brothers living in Maryland (the North), this meant that her family was forced to fight against each other. This news was not only emotionally grievous to Sallie and Landrum, but also impacted them financially. The church was preoccupied with the war in the States, which then prevented them from sending support to the Holmes couple on the mission field in Shanghai.

In 1861, Sallie and Landrum decided to leave Shanghai for a city in China then known as Tengchow. Many people in Tengchow had never heard about Jesus, so that's exactly where this young couple wanted to be. Not long after moving there, their daughter, Annie, got sick. The sickness was unforgiving to the point that their little girl tragically passed away. To make matters even worse, Sallie and Landrum had to travel all the way to a nearby island for her burial because foreigners weren't allowed to be buried on the mainland.

Just three weeks after the Holmes couple buried their only child, word reached the Tengchow people that the rebels of the Taiping Rebellion were on their way to invade their village and destroy everything in sight. Landrum and a few other men decided to approach the rebels, attempt to make peace, and in turn, protect their city. Sallie waited with the people of Tengchow, terrified in the uncertainty of whether all they knew was about to be destroyed and if their own lives were about to be lost.

Time passed, but the rebels didn't attack. Yet Sallie's husband didn't return. Upon investigation, it was learned that Landrum and the men by his side had been brutally murdered by the rebels. When their bodies were found, it was reported that one man couldn't be distinguished from another. After receiving the gut-wrenching news of her husband's horrific death, Sallie realized that Landrum, also a foreigner, had to be buried on the same island where their daughter, Annie, had been laid to rest just weeks prior.

And there she stood. Alone in a town she had only lived in for a handful of months, without her baby and without her husband. Suffering covered her like a blanket.

Just when you might think that there's no way this story could become more complex, it does. Sallie found out that she was pregnant. Imagine being twenty-five years old, having just buried your husband and daughter, and you find that you are alone and pregnant in a foreign nation. In a mere matter of months, she went from having a little girl and a wonderful husband to being a widow who just buried her child and with a baby now on the way.

As Sallie's family and friends were informed of what had happened to Annie and Landrum and that Sallie was with child, they urged her to return home. And they weren't the only ones. The International Mission Board also summoned Sallie to come home. At the time, the board strongly believed that single women were not permitted to be on the mission field, and therefore, they were not going to support her if she stayed.

What was she to do? She had persisted in her faith so well. Now, as sorrow surrounded her and welled up within her, would she persevere? What did perseverance even look like? Being all alone in a village across the ocean from family as she wondered where financial support would come from, she probably felt a million things at once. She likely felt immeasurable love for her baby's face she had yet to see, and also torturous grief for her daughter's face she would give anything to see one more time. She probably felt a shimmer of joy when her baby kicked in her womb, as a tear trickled down her cheek because she wished her husband were there to feel it too.

This was not how she had hoped her story would unfold, yet there she was living in a chapter that felt like a horror story. Mentally, emotionally, physically, and even economically, she was downright burdened. How should she respond to her family? Was her time in China finished? Or would she keep going, even though the difficulties of the terrain had just multiplied?

Going home would have made sense. In fact, if she did, she

would've been welcomed with open arms. Her trip home would have been easier and would have been considered the right thing to do by everyone around her. The trials she was enduring would have been more than valid reasons to back out of the original plan to stay in China. Even responding to this set of circumstances with bitterness toward God for all the adversity she was undergoing would have been understandable to many. After all, she had left the States in obedience to God and arrived in China to experience the loss of her support, the loss of her daughter, and the loss of her husband. Was there even any reason to stay?

In a reply to her loved ones, Sallie wrote:

I wonder if my heart is broken. I hardly know how I do feel. I feel miserable all the time and in agony often. But I know it only seems to be so, and that it really is best just as God has willed it. As far as I know myself, I think I feel unconditional submission to God's will, entire confidence in His love and wisdom, a sort of undefined sense of gratitude to Him for doing what He knows best, though it seems so different to me.[2]

In her heartache, in her uncertainty, in her suffering, she chose to trust God. Trusting Him didn't mean sweeping her emotions under the rug just to get by. She was honest about the emotional condition of her soul, which in turn helped her trust God with the pain that she carried. She kept going in the struggle, believing that God was with her and, even when she didn't understand, that He was working all things together for her good (Romans 8:28).

DEFINING "GOOD"

Walking closely with Jesus, spending time in Scripture, and loving people are things we seem to persist in with ease when life is fairly easy. It's not hard to trust God and serve people when our days are a breeze. But what happens when the sailing is no longer smooth? What happens when life no longer feels like a cushioned, flat track to run around and instead suddenly becomes a mountain to climb? It is this kind of terrain that puts our faith to the test, the kind of terrain that sometimes saps our inspiration. When we are making our way around boulders and heaving up steep slopes in life, we will not always feel like persisting in drawing close to Jesus, abiding in His Word, and loving people. What do we do then? Do we keep working toward our goal or do we pivot because that goal is requiring too much of us?

We may read Sallie's story and wonder, "How could someone who gave up so much for God have so much taken away from her?" Sallie was being so persistent in her faith yet was still experiencing immense grief. Oftentimes we find ourselves believing that these two things cannot go together. Many of us tend to assume that obedience precedes a life of things working out for good—and in a way, this is not wrong. Didn't God Himself say that those who choose the ancient, good paths find rest for their souls (Jeremiah 6:16)? Throughout Scripture we see over and over again that God promises blessings for those who walk with Him.

The problem with our assumption is that we put our own definition on what "good" is. It is common for us to think that God's blessings are supposed to come in a package of ease, health, and many happy moments. We have in our head what we believe God's goodness should look like, so when life begins to press in on us and it feels like everything is falling apart, we become confused. We start to think that the hardship is a sign we aren't where we're supposed to be, as though God only guides us to easy paths. Or in these unmet expectations of what we thought God's goodness looked like, we are tempted to draw away from God and find our personal definition of good elsewhere.

We struggle associating suffering with God because if God works all things together for good, how can walking with God bring suffering? Not only that, but if God works all things together for the good of those who love Him (Romans 8:28), it can be a battle to believe that God loves us when our life isn't looking good. Shouldn't our walk with Him be likened to running around a track rather than traversing terrain that has obstacles and deserts and valleys? We may even find ourselves fervently praying to the Lord about our grievous situation, and we have yet to see our circumstances change. How is it possible that goodness and suffering can be intertwined? We think, *Surely they can't be.*

Jeremiah wrote something to help us reevaluate our definition of good, the good that Sallie seemed to see even in her pain and the good we need to adopt. Penning the words of God, he wrote:

Blessed is the man who trusts in the LORD,
　　whose trust is the LORD.
He is like a tree planted by water,
　　that sends out its roots by the stream,

and does not fear when heat comes,
    for its leaves remain green,
and is not anxious in the year of drought,
    for it does not cease to bear fruit. (Jeremiah 17:7–8)

These verses hold immense contrast. The imagery here is not normal. Plants die in drought. When there is no water to be found, fruit is nonexistent. Yet, the Lord here says that it is possible for goodness to be found in the worst of times. He says that it is possible for life and nourishment to be found in the middle of unbearable heat. In other words, He is telling us how in fact goodness and suffering can be found walking hand in hand.

The goodness reserved for the person who trusts in the Lord is not that they never experience heat or a year of drought. It's not that they get to stay on a smooth, simple path. The goodness God promises is not an avoidance of difficulty. Rather, the goodness lavished on the person who trusts in the Lord is the gift of peace when the drought does come. The goodness looks like having a secure confidence even when the heat settles in. The blessing comes in the form of thriving and flourishing in circumstances where it makes no sense for that to be the case. God has a miraculous way of working the horrid circumstances in life for good by drawing us to Himself amid the pain. He has a sovereign, gracious way of working the gut-wrenching realities of this broken world for the good of our souls and for the good of His glory.

God cares about our circumstances, but even more than our circumstances, He cares about us. He cares about our hearts. He cares about our closeness with Him. God's goodness does not always show up as the instant gratification of seeing everything fall into place. It's even better. His goodness is intimacy with Himself even in the middle of suffering. The goodness He has for us is the gift of being conformed to the likeness of His Son through our suffering. His goodness doesn't always take the pain away, but it gives us the strength to keep going even when the pain is present. His goodness doesn't always change the difficulty of the path we are on, but in His goodness He always invites us to come to Him, take His yoke upon ourselves, and find rest for our souls (Matthew 11:28–30). In His goodness, He draws near to the broken-hearted and He saves the crushed in spirit (Psalm 34:18). His joy, His goodness, is our strength and no sorrow we come face-to-face with could ever separate us from the love of God that is in Christ Jesus (Nehemiah 8:10; Romans 8:37–39). As Sallie said, "He knows best, though it seems so different to me." The hardship she faced did not look best, but she grew closer to Him by trusting that His way is always best.

God's goodness does not always show up as the instant gratification of seeing everything fall into place. It's even better. His goodness is intimacy with Himself even in the middle of suffering.

Not only did submitting to God's will give her hope to stay the course, but she also wrote to her family, saying:

I think I might probably be instrumental in the conversions of more persons at home than here, but if I went home for that and other missionaries acted upon the same principle I doubt if there would be a missionary left in China.[3]

Her goal! The goal of reaching the lost souls in China for the sake of Christ!

EYE ON THE PRIZE

Sallie referred to her reason for coming to China as she responded to the suffering that stared at her dead in the eye. She would persist, not because doing so would be easy, but because her goal mattered more to her than anything else.

When life gets hard, when the days are uphill battles, and we feel as though we are in a middle moment at every turn, may we ask God to show us the bigger picture. May we ask Him to remind us of the direction we are headed amid the mess of suffering. When we call to mind the purpose for boldly living out our faith, our perspective is kept in check. Remembering her goal helped Sallie endure. When we persist in our goal, we will persevere through our suffering.

When we persist in our goal, we will persevere through our suffering.

While studying the life of Sallie Holmes and reflecting on how it is that we endure through hardships, I recalled a childhood memory from my middle school P.E. class. We had a required reoccurring timed mile. To my twelve-year-old self, it was a big deal. Nerves were a close companion all throughout the day of the run, and they escalated with each passing class that indicated I was one step closer to go-time. My heart would pound in my chest as I made my way to the locker room, hoping to get a personal best. I vividly remember my dad encouraging me and helping me prepare for those runs. A piece of advice he shared with me that will stick with me forever was, "Whatever you do, don't stop." He knew there would be moments I would get fatigued. He knew that when it got hard, the strain on my body would make me want to stop. So his simple encouragement was, no matter what, just don't quit.

In the same way, our Heavenly Father is encouraging us. Personally, to you and me, He is championing us to not grow weary of doing good (Galatians 6:9), to finish the race, to keep the faith, and to fight the good fight (2 Timothy 4:7). And how wonderfully profound is it that it is not by our own strength or endurance that we do so, but by *His*? It is *He* who is our very present help in trouble (Psalm 46:1). It is *He* who daily bears our burdens (Psalm 68:19). It is *His* power that is made perfect in our weakness (2 Corinthians 12:9). It is *He* who promises that *He* will bring to completion the good work that *He* started in us (Philippians 1:6). Yes, we have an important part to play, but remember and find relief in the comforting truth that we persevere through our suffering by His strength, and we persist in the goal of living for His glory by His work in us.

Over and over again we see the Lord point us to the end goal as a means of encouraging us to endure through hardships. He continually directs our attention to the finish line to help us keep persevering in the hard, messy, confusing sorrow that life holds. If we keep our sights set on heaven, like Paul pressing on with the aim of telling others the good news about the wonderful grace of God, we will have motivation in our souls to not quit. The suffering we are under as believers is not in vain.

There is an end in sight, and for those who are in Christ Jesus that is absolutely beautiful! This, though, also means that there is an end in sight for those who are not in Christ Jesus, and it is anything but beautiful. With this in mind, it is for the souls of precious people whom God loves that we persevere. In persisting to see many people put their faith in Jesus, we will look at the suffering of this life as more than worth journeying through.

Jesus demonstrated this sacrifice for us when He came upon the week of Passover. Knowing that His time to be crucified was approaching, He said, "Now is my soul troubled. And what shall I say? 'Father, save me from this hour'? But for this purpose I have come to this hour. Father, glorify your name" (John 12:27–28). In the face of suffering, carrying a soul heavy with anxiety, Jesus remembered the goal. He remembered the whole reason He came to earth, and doing so compelled Him to persevere. Not only did Jesus show us how to persevere by persisting in the goal, but He also helps us by empathizing with all we are feeling as we walk through suffering. He gets what it's like to have a broken heart. He understands what it's like to be betrayed by close friends. He knows what it's like when we have lost someone we love so much. No matter what we go through, no matter how hard life gets, Jesus is always filled with sincere awareness of the condition our hearts are in, and He loves us right where we are.

OPPORTUNITY IN THE OBSTACLES

When Sallie decided to stay in China, it was not a short-term decision, nor was it a decision that brought her a greater ease of life. In fact, hard moments continued to follow. She raised her baby boy as a single mother and went through seasons of sickness, all while continuing to serve tirelessly in small towns and villages for the sake of the gospel.

There is a Haitian proverb that reads, "Behind mountains are more mountains." In other words, obstacles in life are not a one-time thing. Life presents numerous and diverse challenges that we must endure, but we should not be taken aback by them. When Peter was writing to the persecuted church, he encouraged them with this:

Do not be surprised at the fiery trial when it comes upon you to test you, as though something strange were happening to you. But rejoice insofar as you share Christ's sufferings, that you may also rejoice and be glad when his glory is revealed. (1 Peter 4:12–13)

The mountains in our lives are not strange, they are to be expected. We are better equipped to persevere through our middle moments when we are prepared for them, when we are alert and of sober mind. Now, what in the world does it look like to prepare for sorrow and suffering when these typically don't give a warning before they come? Though we cannot prepare for them by seeing into the future, knowing exactly when and how those times will arrive, we can prepare by being thoroughly equipped. We prepare ourselves to persevere by relying on what we have persisted in. By persisting in intimacy with Christ, filling our hearts and minds with His Word, and loving people well, we are less likely to be thrown off course when the next mountain is upon us.

It can be rather easy to become discouraged by the thought of more mountains being behind the one we are currently climbing. We can consider this and unintentionally adopt a mindset of merely getting by. But the mountains that make up the land of our lives are not just something we must be ready for. They are also something we need to look at differently.

Instead of seeing that there are more trials ahead of us and taking on a posture of fear, complaining, and defeat, may we adopt the perspective of seeing the suffering that awaits as an opportunity! What if we saw our afflictions as opportunities to grow closer to the heart of God, to trust Him? What if we saw them as reality checks that this life is temporary? What if we saw them as opportunities to be sanctified, to grow to look more like Jesus? What if we embraced the perspective that the fiery trials that come our way are opportunities to experience the joy of the Lord in a way we didn't know possible, and then grasp the depth of Christ's empathy toward us as we've never known?

What if we embraced the perspective that the fiery trials that come our way are opportunities to experience the joy of the Lord in a way we didn't know possible, and then grasp the depth of Christ's empathy toward us as we've never known?

James wrote to the scattered Church:

Count it all joy, my brothers, when you meet trials of various kinds, for you know that the testing of your faith produces steadfastness. And let steadfastness have its full effect, that you may be perfect and complete, lacking nothing. (James 1:2–4)

And again Paul wrote:

We rejoice in our sufferings, knowing that suffering produces endurance, and endurance produces character, and character produces hope, and hope does not put us to shame, because God's love has been poured into our hearts through the Holy Spirit who has been given to us. (Romans 5:3–5)

God not only walks with us through our various sorrows and heartaches, empathizing with us, but He is working purposefully through them too. Our sorrows are opportunities to rejoice because we know that God is doing something good in us for His glory. Though the pain we despise, we can discover comfort in the depths of our souls, knowing God is bringing a good purpose out of it.

This perspective that is anchored in truth changes everything—it changes how we navigate our middle moments and helps us to keep persisting to confidently live out our faith. Suffering never gets easy, but through the work of the Holy Spirit and as we trust in God and persist in the ways of Him, our love for Him overflows more and more with each middle moment we stand in.

As an unsupported, widowed, single mother, Sallie Holmes brought the gospel to "as many as four hundred villages in a year."[4] She and her friend Martha Crawford were reported to have been "tireless in visiting in the city and neighboring villages, giving the Good News in season and out of season."[5] It seems like Sallie only grew more devoted to Jesus as her life went on, like her faith muscles just kept getting stronger with each terrain she trekked with God. She was adamant about the Great Commission. Suffering was not an obstacle that got in the way of her relationship with Christ; rather it was an opportunity for her to grow closer to Him and show people who He was even more.

When Sallie decided to stay in China, her choice didn't only affect her. Many people came to know Christ, and she went on sharing Him with more people even in sorrow. In the same way, when we respond to the middle moments of suffering by persevering and persisting toward our goal, the impact of our choice goes beyond ourselves.

The flourishing we experience by trusting God in drought and intense heat, as Jeremiah wrote, is not only a blessing to us personally but an opportunity to bless others too. There are people around us who are also walking through great trials, but their leaves are withering. They are thirsty and weary as they suffer under the weight of life's circumstances. They are incredibly fearful and anxious as they brace the heat and droughts of life. Then suddenly they catch a glimpse of our decision to keep going with God—like a thriving tree in the middle of a desert. They are taken aback and intrigued by the rest we carry in our souls. Thrown off by how unusual our life looks, they come closer, and discover nourishment, shade, and refreshment by just being around the tree of our life! They cannot help but ask how we are able to have green leaves and bear so much fruit even in times that are so hard. And to their curiosity, we can boldly share about the presence, the glory, and the goodness of God.

As we stand in the middle of unlikely circumstances, we are given the opportunity to share with others where our abundance comes from. Our life is bigger than ourselves. By our suffering, God not only wants to bring about His goodness within us, but also through us to show the world who He is and draw more people to Himself. And isn't this the goal? To deeply know Christ and to love people by showing them who He is? If we remain persistent in the goal, we will continue to persevere through our suffering.

12

Compelled

Christianity, if false, is of no importance and, if true, is of infinite importance. The one thing it cannot be is moderately important.

—C. S. Lewis

Throughout the pages of this book we have looked at the lives of multiple people who were given the opportunity to decide which way they would go when they reached a crossroads—a middle moment. From Michelangelo deciding if he would embark on the journey of carving the statue of David, to Amy Carmichael deciding if she would go to a place she had never been, each had a cost to count before making their choice. From Moses considering if he would go to Pharaoh, to Thomas Edison determining if he would persist in inventing the incandescent lightbulb, both had an opportunity to go one way or the other.

Each of these people came face-to-face with middle moments, just as we do every single day. Every day we are given opportunities to make decisions—not just decisions on what we will have for lunch or what we will wear, but with each new sunrise we get to choose if we will boldly live out our faith or not.

As we stand in the balance of concluding whether we will follow God into the unknown, we are standing in a middle moment, an opportunity to choose Him. When we know that mockery and rejection will come our way if we decide to be unashamed about our love for Jesus, before us lies an opportunity, an invitation from God to go with Him. When the terrain of our life goes from smooth to rocky and we are contemplating persevering in faith, we are at the foot of a mountainous opportunity to trust God.

Yet even after reading this book and committing to walk with God today, we will still encounter temptations to take a different path. A distorted view of God will continually try to claim a place in our thoughts. The world will want to shape our idea of what God is like. It will be tempting to let our circumstances determine our level of confidence instead of God.

Excuses will not stop presenting themselves. Excuses are a lack of faith disguised as being realistic and humble, and they will still want a say in our middle moments. When we hear God's call to step out in faith, reminders of our disqualifications will linger in our minds. Doubts about our own capability will press in on our hearts. Memories of how our past ought to keep us from what God wants to do in the future will be recalled.

The way of comfort and ease will not entirely become unattractive. Instant gratification will still look desirable and there will be times we will want to go in its direction. Fear will not disappear. It will continue trying to stir up panic, saying, "Turn around! Following Jesus is too risky!" These feelings don't go away when we choose Christ in a middle moment, but they will persist in the many middle moments to follow. They will continue to speak up and make themselves known when we are daily considering the direction we should go. The excuses, the fear, and the desire for comfort might try to have a say in our response, but at the end of the day, we are the ones who get to decide which way we are going to go.

WE MUST CHOOSE

Our everyday middle moments show up in a variety of ways. They look like waking up with a family who doesn't believe in Jesus. They look like moving into a new neighborhood full of people we have never met, starting a new job with new coworkers we now see every day, or joining a sorority with girls from many different walks of life. They take the form of mundane routines in daily marriage and motherhood. They show up as we experience grief and pain and heartache. They look like getting cyberbullied while sitting in the bleachers at a basketball game, and they look like considering what to do after hearing the Lord has called us to proclaim the gospel overseas.

Middle moments show up when we are face-to-face with the cashier while checking out our groceries, and middle moments take on the form of seeing the same people at the gym week in and week out. Many of these moments don't even sound monumental. Maybe we read these moments and are confused about what decision even needs to be made in them. That's the whole point. Most of the time, middle moments go without notice in our days, and it is time that we see them for the impactful, significant opportunities they are. Whether we are aware of it or not, we have been making decisions every day because our middle moments require a response.

We cannot have our cake and eat it too. We cannot stand at a fork in the road and go both ways. We cannot choose light and darkness. There is no middle ground in our middle moments; we have to make a decision. Jesus said, "Whoever is not with me is against me" (Matthew 12:30). Will we choose Christ, or will we choose our fear and love of comfort? Neutral is not an option.

In our response, will we let the fear and excuses and love of comfort call the shots? Fear wants us to respond by never bringing up Jesus with our unbelieving family because it could stir up conflict. And, on top of that, what if we stumble in our words? When we respond in fear, we don't let our light shine before those in our sorority or at our workplace because they could respond by thinking we are weird. Fear lies to us, causing us to doubt if there is any real significance in sharing the love of Christ amid our mundane routines in the four walls of our home with our spouse and kids. Fear leads us to conform, grow timid, and be rooted in insecurity when reading the mocking, hateful comments at the basketball game.

Excuses want us to respond to our middle moments by never reaching out to those in the neighborhood because we are too busy. Excuses lead us to rush through our encounter with the cashier because we don't have time to ask them how they are doing.

Instant gratification wants us to stay in the immediate comfort of our own home rather than follow God's call to move overseas. In an interesting way it wants us to turn from God in our sorrow because persevering in trust seems too hard.

Desire for comfort keeps us to ourselves at the gym because it takes too much energy to get to know those around us. It draws us away from doing anything we just don't feel like doing.

Fear will try to keep us safe. Excuses will work their hardest to make us avoid the task at hand. Instant gratification will intensely attempt to persuade us to stay comfortable. But there is danger on the path of the Christian walk. There are eternally important tasks to be done. There is delayed gratification to be eagerly awaited as instant comfort is sacrificed. We cannot live with a fearful, excuse-driven, comfortable Christian mentality while also boldly living out our faith. It's one or the other.

Responding to our middle moments by boldly living out our faith looks like walking with Jesus daily. It looks like talking with Him, spending time with Him, and walking hand in hand with His friends as we face trials and temptations. It looks like being a good neighbor to even the hard-to-love people. It looks like showing grace to the bullies and clinging to what He has spoken when their mocking words are blaring. It looks like praying for our family members who don't know Him and loving them well in word and in deed even when it is hard. It looks like leaning into the not-so-glamorous everyday opportunities to love our spouse and kids like Jesus.

Putting our faith to action looks like initiating hospitality instead of waiting for our neighbors to come to us. It looks like being an imitator of Christ among our peers and colleagues even if they don't agree with the faith we have. It looks like walking by faith even when the excuses and desire for comfort are emphatic.

Responding with bold faith in our middle moments looks like showing up at the gym and the grocery store and our other everyday places to encourage people even if it means going out of our way, willing to be inconvenienced and interrupted. God allows opportunities to come our way so that we might make the most of them. But to make the most of them, we have to respond to them by boldly living out our faith in Him.

Jesus said, "If anyone would come after me, let him deny himself and take up his cross daily and follow me" (Luke 9:23). Choosing Christ is a daily decision, and most of the time, it is not comfortable. Denying ourselves is not fun. To take up our cross is to carry the most gruesome, weighty death. This daily followership of Jesus requires that fear and excuses and instant gratification no longer have the final say in which direction we go. This is why there is no middle ground. This is why you and I must choose daily how we will respond to our middle moments.

WHAT IF?

What if we started to see our middle moments as opportunities to live out our faith boldly rather than either as not important enough to matter, or as obstacles in our way to dodge and ignore? Not only that, but what if we started specifically asking God for those opportunities? I bet we would have a change in perspective of our current circumstances. I am confident that we would begin to live with intention in the mundane hours of our days, alert and ready to bless whoever we came across. We would see the eternal purpose of our current position, wherever that may be.

Reflecting on Jesus's command to "go and make disciples of all nations" (Matthew 28:19, NIV), Bible commentator Stuart Weber wrote:

> *Going* means more than traveling across geographical borders, although this is part of Jesus's meaning. The point is that we believers are active; we are not inert. *Going* means crossing boundaries to make disciples—going across the street, going to dinner with an unbelieving friend, going into the inner city, going beyond one's comfort zone to make the gospel accessible to the lost. Living life is "going" with a purpose, every day.[1]

When we go and make disciples, we are choosing to respond in our middle moments with bold faith lived out.

What if we started asking God to help us make the most of the opportunities right in front of us? This is what Paul did. In his letter to the church of Colossae, he wrote:

> Pray for us . . . that God will give us many opportunities to speak about his mysterious plan concerning Christ. That is why I am here in chains. Pray that I will proclaim this message as clearly as I should. Live wisely among those who are not believers, and make the most of every opportunity. (Colossians 4:3–6, NLT)

Paul asked the church to pray that God would give him opportunities to share Jesus with others. He asked them to pray for him to make the most of the opportunities he was given, and he encouraged them to do likewise. Not to mention, he did all this while in prison! Paul was sitting in a jail cell focusing on how he could best steward his time there, sharing the gospel with anyone he could. He was not waiting to get out of shackles to share. He trusted God would use him and be glorified through him in the very position he was in.

Paul was exemplifying to us through his own life that we need not wait for "ideal" moments to make the most of our faith. Rarely will there ever be what feels like a perfect time to step out of our comfort zone, face our fears, and live sacrificially. Most of the time, being bold will not be easy. More often than not, the situations God positions us in to so daringly walk with Him will not appear perfectly nice and neat. We have not been called to start living for God once we have reached a certain point in life, are in a certain season, or feel a certain way. We have been called to respond to the opportunities He gives us by going with Him right now by the power of His Spirit.

Another way of putting what Paul wrote would be to pray for middle moments. Pray for opportunities to grow closer to Christ. Pray for opportunities to bless people richly. Pray for opportunities to proclaim the gospel and bring immense glory to God and make the most of those opportunities by choosing Christ when they come.

HERE'S WHY

The question we all find ourselves asking at some point, though, is "Why?" What is the point of noticing our middle moments and responding to them with bold faith? Why does any of it even matter? If there are more comfortable routes, why intentionally choose the route that requires complete abandon? This is a beautiful question and is necessary to answer because the answer to this question is what keeps us going even when it is challenging. Knowing the answer to this question is what fuels us with hope. It's what guards us from growing weary and strengthens us to persevere in making the most of every opportunity for the sake of Christ. It is when we recall the answer to the question "Why?" that we will be ignited with passion to press on in faith.

Paul wrote to the Corinthian church:

> For Christ's love compels us, because we are convinced that one died for all, and therefore all died. And he died for all, that those who live should no longer live for themselves but for him who died for them and was raised again. (2 Corinthians 5:14–15, NIV)

The love of Christ is our reason! His love is our answer. Without His love displayed in His death, burial, and resurrection, none of this even matters. But because His love was perfectly demonstrated and overcame death, hell, and the grave, nothing matters more!

Scripture says that "if Christ has not been raised, our preaching is useless and so is your faith" (1 Corinthians 15:14, NIV). In other words, if the gospel is not true, there is no need for us to boldly live out our faith as we stand in middle moments. Yet Scripture goes on to say, "But Christ has indeed been raised from the dead" and because of this, the only fitting response to our middle moments is to no longer live for ourselves, but to live zealously for Him (1 Corinthians 15:20, NIV).

As mentioned in the beginning of our journey together, the word "compel" means to urge or motivate someone to do something. The most fitting response to give when we experience the love of Christ is to take action in bold faith, to be motivated to make the most of every opportunity, and to live with a sense of urgency about the things of heaven. To be driven by this love means that we stop living for excuses and start walking by faith. To be urged on by the love of Christ means that we stop ignoring sacrifices to maintain ease and start going with Him unconditionally. Living constrained and completely enraptured by the love of Christ means that we stop letting our circumstances dominate our perception of God and start letting His promises shape our perspective.

The most fitting response to give when we experience the love of Christ is to take action in bold faith, to be motivated to make the most of every opportunity, and to live with a sense of urgency about the things of heaven.

Being all in for Christ means that approval, or lack thereof, from people is no longer our motivation for living the life we do; only His approval is. It means that we are radically on a mission to seize every opportunity we are given to share this love with everyone we possibly can. The only prerequisite for living compelled by the love of Christ is to be a child of God. The moment we put our faith in Christ is the moment we can begin to live compelled by His love. We don't have to wait until we have more experience under our belt. We don't have to wait until we know more of His Word. We don't have to have a certain past or a certain personality. If we have Christ's love, we have everything we need to boldly live out our faith.

If we have Christ's love, we have everything we need to boldly live out our faith.

The reason why the love of Christ keeps us going even when it's hard and even when there are unknowns and even when people don't like us for it is because the love of Christ is unfailing and unending. When we are at our wits' end and don't feel as though we have the strength or the capacity to continue choosing the ancient, good path in our middle moments, it is the love of Christ that sustains us. It is the love of Christ that holds up our head so we can be reminded of the goal.

Notice that Paul didn't say his reason for boldly living out his faith was because he needed to just do the best he could at following God's commands, nor did he say that it was because his own love for Christ compelled him. If this were the case, his ministry would have fizzled out because Paul's endurance would have been based on his own energy, his own efforts. Commentator Warren Wiersbe wrote that when Paul said he was compelled by the love of Christ, he was not saying that he was compelled by his own "love for Christ, although certainly that was there." Wiersbe maintained, rather, that Paul was compelled by "the love Christ had for [him]."[2] The love of Jesus was Paul's reason for leveraging his whole life for the gospel, and because of that, he kept going to the end.

Responding to our middle moments with confident faith is not something we can do by our own might. It is only by the power of the Holy Spirit compelling us with Christ's love that we can be steadfast in making the most of every opportunity. This is not a call to be a better person or a call to try harder to live out our faith. This is a call to live for Christ as we depend on Christ. Nothing about this can be done apart from Him. Before Christ told us to go and make disciples of all nations, He said that we are to do so confidently resting in this: that "All authority in heaven and on earth has been given to [Him]" (Matthew 28:18, NIV).

We can make the most of our middle moments knowing how all of this ends. Christ wins! He is on the throne! We can unapologetically live out our faith knowing that it is not in vain because all authority has been given to Him. Not only that, but we can know that as we stand in our middle moments every single day, we don't stand alone. For He is with us "always, to the very end of the age" (Matthew 28:20, NIV). So as you rely on the God who is with you and holds all victory, may you respond in your middle moments compelled by the love of Christ!

ACKNOWLEDGMENTS

I know that acknowledgments are often neglected to be read in a book, but I feel so strongly that these pages are some of the most important. For without these people, this book would not be what it is, and I would not be who I am. What an honor to acknowledge these significant people in my life who have prayed with me, encouraged me, called me higher, served me, and exemplified astoundingly what it means to live out the words written in this book.

To begin, I praise You, God. Thank You for loving me perfectly. Thank You for sending Your one and only Son, Jesus, to save me that I may know You. Living compelled by Your love that is better than life is my greatest joy. Thank You for strengthening my faith and for deepening my intimacy with You in unexpected and undreamed-of ways through the writing of this book.

Josh, the Lord has gifted me with the honor of having you as my husband, teammate, and best friend. In the process of this book being written, you saw it all. You saw when the dream was first placed on my heart in college. You saw when I wanted to quit. You saw when I celebrated. You saw when I wrestled. You wiped the tears that streamed down my face over and over again when the doubt and discouragement were heavy. Within the four walls of our home, you witnessed my faith journey amid many terrains. So graciously and ever patiently, you prayed for me, you believed in God with me, and you championed me in the truth. I think this book would still be just a Word doc if not for your loving support. I praise God for you and love you more than I could ever find the words to express.

My dearest Margot, though you are a baby, you inspire me immensely to embrace the message written in these pages. You know very few words, but your life speaks volumes. Thank you for being a continual reminder to me that my life is bigger than me. Thank you for building me up in the truth that God has generations and legacies in mind for the glory of His name. I pray that you may grasp how deep and high and long and wide God's unfailing love is for you, and that this love may compel you your whole life. What a privilege to be your mom.

To my incredible family, thank you for teaching me about the love of Jesus through word and deed. Thank you for the many, many times that you rearranged your schedules to watch Margot so that I could pen the words that make up this book. In countless ways through different seasons in my life, you have pointed me to Christ and shown me what it really means to follow Him no matter what. Each of you has such a special place in my heart, and I am so grateful that you are the people I get to do daily life with.

To my friends, those of you who live right down the road and those of you who live across state lines, I love you deeply. You are a refreshment to me and have, over and over again, reminded me of what matters most. Thank you for praying with me and for cheering me on. Life with each of you is so much fun and I rejoice in the Lord for the gift of my people.

Kathleen Kerr, you have been a powerhouse of encouragement from the beginning. You are not just my agent, you are my friend and fellow sister in Christ. I am thankful for your kindness, for your love for God, and for your devotion to His Word. You are a testament to God's provision in my life, and you saw the Lord's hand on me when I didn't feel it. Thank you for believing in me, for praying for me, and for wholeheartedly jumping into this journey with me.

Xochitl Dixon, every time I sit down to write I think about you because you were the one who, in high school, taught me to never start writing until I first pray. Hours upon hours you have sacrificed to help me walk in a manner worthy of the calling I have received. Not only have you taught me how to be a better writer, but more than anything you have taught me how to depend on God. Thank you for setting such a beautiful example for me to see what it looks like to trust in Him. Thank you for affirming me in the gifts that God has given me. Your investment in my life is an eternal one, and I am ever grateful.

My beloved team at WaterBrook, I praise God for your sincerity, diligence, and passion to help me communicate this message and reach as many people with it as possible. You are compelled to give all glory to God, and I am honored that we would get to do this fun, significant work together.

NOTES

CHAPTER 1: MIDDLE MOMENTS

1. J. I. Packer, *Knowing God* (InterVarsity Press, 2023), 38.
2. Tracy Munsil, "What Does It Mean When People Say They Are 'Christian'?" Cultural Research Center, tinyurl.com/5n8ju7xk.
3. Munsil, "What Does It Mean When People Say They Are 'Christian'?"
4. C. S. Lewis, *The Complete C. S. Lewis Signature Classics* (Harper One, 2002), 155.

CHAPTER 2: CHANGE OF PERSPECTIVE

1. "Carrara: The Capital of Marble That Remembers Michelangelo," Bella Vista Collection, bellavistacollection.com/carrara-the-capital-of-marble-that-remembers-michelangelo/.
2. "Michelangelo's David," Analysis of the Art of Renaissance Italy, tinyurl.com/4nfpmhe2.
3. Howard E. Lewine, "Understanding the Stress Response," Harvard Health Publishing, health.harvard.edu/staying-healthy/understanding-the-stress-response.

4. Ann Marie Menting, "The Chill of Fear," *Harvard Medicine*, Summer 2011, magazine.hms.harvard.edu/articles/chill-fear.

5. A. W. Tozer, *The Knowledge of the Holy* (Harper Collins, 1961), 1.

CHAPTER 3: EXCUSES

1. Shel Silverstein, *Where the Sidewalk Ends: Poems and Drawings* (HarperCollins Children's, 1974), 38.

2. Douglas Stuart, *Exodus, The New American Commentary* (Broadman & Holman Publishers, 2006), 113.

3. "Hudson Taylor," *Christianity Today*, August 2008, christianitytoday.com/2008/08/hudson-taylor/.

4. Warren W. Wiersbe, *Be Delivered (Exodus), The BE Series Commentary* (Cook Communications Ministries, 1998), 24.

CHAPTER 4: THE COMFORTABLE CHRISTIAN

1. Jennifer Leavitt, "How Much Deep, Light, and REM Sleep Do You Need?" healthline, January 18, 2024, healthline.com/health/how-much-deep-sleep-do-you-need.

2. Keiko Ogawa, Emi Kaizuma-Ueyama, and Mitsuo Hayashi, "Effects of Using a Snooze Alarm on Sleep Inertia after Morning Awakening," *Journal of Physiological Anthropology* 41, no. 1 (December 2022), doi.org/10.1186/s40101-022-00317-w.

3. "Circadian Rhythm," Cleveland Clinic, my.clevelandclinic .org/health/articles/circadian-rhythm#:~:text=If%20 adults%20practice%20healthy%20habits,changing%20as%20 they%20get%20older.

CHAPTER 5: A PERSONAL RELATIONSHIP

1. Haley DiMarco, *Devotions for the God Girl* (Baker Publishing Group, 2010), v.
2. William Barclay, *The Gospel of Matthew,* vol. 2 (Publications in India, 2009), 161.
3. Michael Reeves, *Rejoice and Trembling* (Crossway, 2021), 16.
4. C. H. Spurgeon, "A Fear to Be Desired," in *The Metropolitan Tabernacle Pulpit Sermons,* 63 vols. (Passmore & Alabaster, 1855–1917), 48:496.

CHAPTER 6: IT IS WRITTEN

1. Adam Macinnis, "Report: 26 Million Americans Stopped Reading the Bible Regularly During COVID-19," *Christianity Today,* April 2022, christianitytoday.com/2022/04/state-of-bible-reading-decline-report-26-million/.
2. Kaitlin Woolley and Marissa A. Sharif, "The Psychology of Your Scrolling Addiction," *Harvard Business Review,* January 2022, hbr.org/2022/01/the-psychology-of-your-scrolling-addiction.
3. Robert A. Traina, *Methodical Bible Study* (Zondervan, 1952), 33.
4. Simon Kemp, "The Time We Spend on Social Media," Data-Reportal, tinyurl.com/ywbymr9u.

CHAPTER 7: WHO IS MY NEIGHBOR?

1. Lawrence O. Richards, *The Teacher's Commentary,* Bible Commentary (Scripture Press Publications, 1987), 132.

CHAPTER 8: WHEN THEY LIKE YOU

1. Saul McLeod, "Solomon Asch Conformity Line Experiment Study," *Simply Psychology,* simplypsychology.org/asch -conformity.html.

CHAPTER 9: AND WHEN THEY DON'T

1. Robert Frost, "The Road Not Taken" (1915), 18–20.
2. Matthew Henry, *Matthew Henry's Commentary on the Whole Bible: Complete and Unabridged in One Volume* (Hendrickson, 1994), 2126.
3. Abby Gardner, "All the Biggest Moments from the New Taylor Swift Documentary, Miss Americana," glamour.com/story/ taylor-swift-miss-americana-review.
4. Donald Guthrie, *Hebrews: An Introduction and Commentary,* vol. 15, Tyndale New Testament Commentaries (InterVarsity Press, 1983), 251.
5. Raj Raghunathan, "How Not to Worry About What Others Think of You," *Psychology Today,* March 2016, psychologytoday.com/us/blog/sapient-nature/201603/how -not-worry-about-what-others-think-you.

CHAPTER 10: GO WHEN YOU DON'T KNOW

1. Abigail Brenner, "5 Benefits of Stepping Outside Your Comfort Zone," *Psychology Today,* December 2015, psychologytoday.com/intl/blog/in-flux/201512/5-benefits-of -stepping-outside-your-comfort-zone.

CHAPTER 11: GO WHEN IT'S HARD

1. "Edison's Lightbulb," The Franklin Institute, tinyurl.com/ 4wbd83u5.

2. Ross Paterson, "Sallie Holmes and the Word of the Holy Spirit in Mission," Field Partner International, staging.fieldpartner .org/resources/articles/sallie-holmes-the-work-of-the-holy -spirit-in-mission/.

3. Scott Peterson, "Even Lottie Moon Had a Mentor in Missions: Meet Sallie Holmes," International Mission Board, imb.org/2017/03/15/sallie-holmes/.

4. Peterson, "Even Lottie Moon Had a Mentor in Missions: Meet Sallie Holmes."

5. Peterson, "Even Lottie Moon Had a Mentor in Missions: Meet Sallie Holmes."

CHAPTER 12: COMPELLED

1. Stuart K. Weber, *Holman New Testament Commentary: Matthew* (Holman Reference, 2000), 484.

2. Warren W. Wiersbe, *Wiersbe's Expository Outlines on the New Testament* (Victor Books, 1992), 489.

ABOUT THE AUTHOR

EMMA MAE MCDANIEL is the founder of Compelled Ministries, a nonprofit organization that helps women personally know the love of Jesus and equips them to boldly live out their faith in Him. She is an author, speaker, and podcast host who is living on a mission to lead this generation to live compelled by Christ's love. Traveling to preach God's Word excites her to the core, and she stewards her social media platforms to reach and encourage people all over the globe. The *Compelled* podcast, with more than five million listens, releases an episode weekly in which McDaniel creates a space to teach her listeners about God and show them how to apply His Word to their lives. She is the author of several books, including *Be Loved, All-Caps You,* and *You Are.*

Emma Mae McDaniel is currently studying at Dallas Theological Seminary to earn a master's degree in Christian education. She and her husband, Josh, live in Bentonville, Arkansas, with their daughter, Margot.